PATRICK T. GRADY

PATRICK T. GRADY

Who Packs The Parachute?

WHO PACKS THE PARACHUTE?

Patrick T. Grady

Copyright 1999
Library of Congress Catalog Card Number: 99-071497
ISBN #: 0-9662361-1-4

Published by:
H.O.P.E. Inc. Press
118 East Lawyers Rd.
Monroe, NC 28110

To purchase additional copies of
WHO PACKS THE PARACHUTE?
contact *"TNT"* Enterprises, Inc.
(800) 862-1660

DEDICATION

This book is dedicated to the light of my life, my wife, Rozanne and our children Brittani Marie, Ashley Rose and Brandon Patrick. You have made my life complete and my world brighter. You are a true joy and I love you all deeply.

ACKNOWLEDGMENTS

William E. and Myrna S. Grady (my parents). Thanks for the sacrifices you made and the foundation you laid for all of your children. I am who I am because of you both.

Terry, Ed, Eileen, Bill, Myrna, Kathleen (my brothers and sisters). Thanks for your faith in me and for listening to all my stories. You are the greatest audience in the world.

Robert & Anatolia Papuga (my in-laws). It has been said that behind every successful man, is a set of surprised in-laws . . . I hope one day to surprise you. Thank you for your continued belief in what I do and for your constant encouragement.

Glenn & Patricia Wade. I am forever grateful for your constant support, guidance and friendship. Thank you for all you have done.

Farier M. Wade. Thanks for the positive influence you have been on me and for "jerking a knot in my tail" when I needed it.

Chuck & Kim Brannan, Clay & Bridget Carmichael, Ryan & Coleen Cox, Jim & Tina Koutsky, John & Michelle Marti and Al & Donna Mazzola. If true friends are a treasure, I am a rich man.

To Randy Keith Kilby (1955 - 1997). My hero, my friend! You are missed.

Jones, Lisa and Alexandria Loflin. Thanks for your friendship, support and all the work you've done to make this book a reality.

Dr. Lamar Simmons. My appreciation for you cannot be measured. Thank you for the opportunity to make my dream come true.

Steve N. Handley, Lynne P. Long and all the teachers who have molded me into the person I am today. Thanks for all you have done to prepare me and others for a tremendous future. You're the best!

Past, present and future clients. I am thankful to each of you for providing me the opportunity to live my dreams.

CONTENTS

FOREWORD

"Generally Speaking," I have spoken to literally hundreds of audiences nationwide. This experience has provided me an opportunity to gather thoughts, opinions and innovative approaches to life from a great many individuals. In *Who Packs The Parachute,* I have attempted to blend stories, insights, and information from keynote addresses and workshops with many of the ideas shared with me by audience members.

As you read this book, you will find that each individual chapter is a collection of thoughts on getting the most out of life as we pursue our goals, for it is often in the pursuit of our dreams that we create our greatest memories and satisfactions. It is these recollections that are the most significant gifts of life.

As parents and business professionals, we are constantly **"Investing In Futures."** Whether it is the future of our children or our associates, we are **"The Custodian"** of their tomorrows. **"The Question Is . . ."** are we contributing to their lives positively or negatively? As we deal with helping to create the futures of others, we occasionally need **"An Attitude Adjustment!"** We must constantly strive to **"Breakthrough"** the obstacles of life in order to get the greatest returns on our investments. We can do this by creating a positive, educational experience for those with whom we come into contact.

Being a parent and a professional can be overwhelming at times. However, we can learn a great deal from our children as well as our associates.

Recently, I was giving my three-year-old daughter Brittani a bath. I turned my back momentarily, and when I faced her again she had an empty bottle of "Baby Magic" soap in her hand. Only thirty seconds earlier this had been a full bottle. Brittani had squirted the contents of the plastic jug into the tub and was busy stirring the water, attempting to create a mountain of bubbles. Of course, being the father, the time came to discipline her and try to explain why dumping an entire bottle of soap into the tub was wasteful. My irritation showed not only in my voice but apparently in my motions. I said, "Brittani, you don't do that! You have just wasted a whole bottle of soap by pouring it all into the tub. You only need a few drops and now it's all gone. Mommy and daddy have to buy a new bottle tomorrow, and this is a waste of money. Don't do this again!"

I felt as though I had done a pretty good job of explaining myself when she looked up at me, batted her big brown eyes, and said, "Don't be mad, Daddy . . . it's only soap!" (Of course I laughed!)

"From The Mouths of Babes" comes the wisdom of the ages. It's only soap! A number of the strenuous, irritating, stressful situations we encounter on a daily basis are likewise only soap. They can bring tears to our eyes but leave us refreshed when they pass. When tomorrow comes, we will see how insignificant they were.

Here's **"One For The Road."** Let's head down the highway to success with a great attitude. If we invest in our minds and the minds of those relying upon us, the return will be ten fold. With the right attitude, our free-fall into life can be everything we want it to be and more.

AN
ATTITUDE
ADJUSTMENT

An Attitude Adjustment

My wife Rozanne and I both taught middle and high school for a number of years and experienced many of the stresses that working with young people can bring. However, that experience does not hold a candle to the joys, satisfactions, challenges, and rewards of being parents. The job of being a mom and dad is one of the most fascinating and overwhelming things that we have ever done. After four and one half years of treatment for infertility, my wife and I were blessed with the birth of our first child, Brittani Marie. Twenty months later and after an additional year of infertility, our twins Ashley Rose and Brandon Patrick made their way into the world.

No one could ever prepare us for the adventure we were about to undertake and the amount of time, patience, love, diapers, and formula that these precious children demand. We quickly found that the term "sleep like a baby" meant that they wake up every thirty minutes all night long, crying.

In the Bible, the difficulties of being parents are addressed numerous times. In one passage, God even asked Abraham to sacrifice his son. Why did God ask him to sacrifice his *young* son? Because, if Abraham waited until the child was a teenager, it might not have been a sacrifice!

As we reflect on the many trials and tribulations of being moms and dads, we often find that some of the situations that cause us the greatest irritation and stress, after a period of time, become our fondest memories. But we must be aware of the words we speak to our children and try to be as encouraging as we possibly can. We must guide and direct them. Give constructive criticism as well as positive feedback. *Like us, our children will make mistakes, but if we help them learn from their mistakes then they become lessons.*

We can turn on our televisions, listen to our radios, and read our newspapers on a daily basis, and hear and read countless reports on the terrible things that are happening in our communities and the tragic things some people are experiencing. Rarely do we hear about the contributions people are making to their neighborhoods and towns. Sadly, we seem to live in a society that more and more everyday sensationalizes immoral behavior and makes media sensations out of thugs.

My experience as an educator and as a speaker is that the vast majority of the people in our country are good. Ninety nine percent of the people in our homes, businesses, and schools are decent, caring individuals that will go out of their way to help others. Wouldn't it be wonderful to bring the attention to those people that they so richly deserve?

Our job as parents is to raise descent, responsible, independent, thinking children who will contribute to their communities. One tool that is available to each of us, in completing this task, is the ability to find the talents and skills that our children possess. We can then nurture and support our children by helping them to grow and develop each of their special abilities. One very simple method is to use our ability to speak. Be aware, however, that the tongue is like fire, and fire is a tool that can be used for good or evil.

We can choose to be people builders or people breakers. Yes, it is simply a choice. (Be aware, O little tongue, be aware of what we say and how we say it!)

I have compiled a humorous look at some of the things we sometimes say to our children. You may be able to identify and relate to many of the statements.

- ◆ Now you listen here, and don't make me repeat myself!
- ◆ If I've told you once, I've told you a thousand times, clean up this room!

- How in the world can you stand to sit in this "pig- sty?"
- Don't you roll your eyes at me.
- I'll make your head roll.
- I'll beat you until you can't grow anymore.
- Going to tell me you're not going to do something when I tell you to do something?
- You move when I say move!
- If you think that I was put on this earth to be your slave, you've got another thing coming.
- Day and night, night and day, I work my fingers to the bone. For what?
- Don't you talk back to me.
- You keep your mouth shut.
- You be quiet when I ask you a question.
- Think I'm talking to hear myself talk? Answer me!
- As long as you live under my roof, you'll follow my rules.
- When I say jump, you say, how high?
- I am sick and tired of hearing you complain.
- You've got it easy.
- You think that money grows on trees.
- I work hard to give you all the things I never had.
- Why, when I was your age we had to walk to school, through the rain, snow, sleet and hail, seven miles, up hill, BOTH ways! Barefooted!
- Oh, stop your whining!
- Would you like something to cry about?
- I'll give you something to cry about.

- This spanking is going to hurt me more than it hurts you.
- You really know how to get under my skin.
- Where did you learn that?
- Do you do everything your friends do?
- If your friend jumped off a bridge, would you jump off a bridge?
- You're not listening.
- When are you going to grow up?
- Get a job!
- Take out the garbage!
- Feed the dog and stay out of the cookies, you'll spoil your dinner!
- Clean your plate!
- Do you know that there are people in this world who are starving to death?
- Oh, just go to bed.
- Why? Because, I said so.
- Take a shower, brush your teeth, flush the toilet, and hurry up!
- I hope you don't act this way in public. Do you?
- Don't you lie to me!
- You know I wasn't born yesterday.
- Hey, you know I'm only doing this for your own good.
- Some day you'll thank me for it.
- And I hope, I truly, truly hope that your children act just like you!

Bill Cosby said his father set things straight in the very beginning by saying, "Son, I brought you into this world, I'll take you out and your mother and I will make another one that looks just like you!"

How many of these statements were you able to complete? How many of these statements have you heard? How many have we ourselves said? Did you just say to yourself, "Oh no! I've become my parents!" (One of the perks of being parents is that we get to carry on the tradition and pass these "ditties" on to our own children.)

I did not write these statements to pick on parents, nor is it my intention to humiliate moms and dads. But it is amazing to hear elementary students say these along with me and see corporate executives hiding their faces in their hands thinking I'd just left their homes. I see the smiles on the faces of middle and high school students as we share them in unison or hear the laughter of adults as we hear ourselves. I do, in a humorous way, want us to think about some of the things we say to others. We should examine our attitudes and reflect upon the words we speak.

Our verbalizations can encourage, support, and motivate others, or they can destroy them. If I had a child, friend, acquaintance or co-worker standing in front of me and said, "You are stupid! You can't do anything right! You are so dumb!" How many times would I have to say these things before they would believe them? Probably once. On the other hand, how often do we need to provide words of encouragement to build positive self-esteem in others and to affect their attitudes in a beneficial fashion? Constantly!

You should never forget that you never know to whom you are speaking when you speak with a child. That child, in the future, could be the surgeon looking into your eyes as you lay on the operating table as the patient. Wouldn't it be tremendously rewarding to know that you did the best by him or her? We do not know the potential of another, but if we take the time to guide and direct others, there is no telling what he or she can become.

We would never, ever allow anyone to come into our homes and take away our possessions. Don't ever let anyone come into your hearts or minds or those of your children or associates and take away their goals and dreams! Goals and dreams are truly the treasures of our futures.

There is an old story you may be familiar with that goes something like this:

A man and his wife pulled into the full-service island at a service station to fill their gas tank during a long vacation trip. The attendant came out to fill up the tank and initiated a conversation with the gentleman behind the wheel. The attendant said, "I noticed by your license plate that you are from New York." "Yes, we are," said the driver. "We're on vacation." In a very bitter voice the wife said,

"What did he say?" "He said, he noticed that we were from New York," replied the husband. "Oh," she said. The worker said, "I used to know some people from New York City." Again, the woman yelled, "What did he say?" The husband responded, "He said he used to know some people from New York City." "Oh," she said. "Actually, I used to work for those people," the attendant added. The wife snapped, "What did he say?" "He said he used to work for some people from New York City." "Oh," she said. The attendant continued, "You know those people never had anything good to say about anyone or any job we did. They constantly ridiculed others and were extremely negative. So negative, in fact, they could give an Alka Seltzer heartburn!" "What did he say," asked the woman? The husband replied, "He said he thinks he knows you!"

As we try to be the best parents, siblings, teachers, students, managers, and people that we can be, take heed that occasionally we will meet people who seem to be full of pessimism.

Sadly enough we meet people with this type of outlook everyday. In both our personal and professional lives, we meet individuals who seem miserable with everyone and everything they do. Some individuals are so set in their ways that nothing you or I try to do seems to have any effect. I firmly believe that we can only influence people. We cannot change them. Change is something that comes from within when a person consciously works on redirecting their thoughts and mindset. Again, however, our influence upon that person or persons can assist them to develop, for example, a more positive, optimistic outlook on life.

To help you to be more optimistic about life, I challenge you to get an index card. Sit down by yourself in a quiet area. Reflect on both your personal and professional life. On this index card, write down a word or two that will remind you of your fondest memories, your greatest accomplishments and achievements. Continue to add to this list on a weekly or monthly basis. When you are feeling down, overwhelmed, or just plain burned out, take the list out of your wallet or purse and reflect upon all the blessings you've received.

Wouldn't it be wonderful if we could forget our troubles as quickly as we forget our blessings?

Try to make the best of bad situations. When something happens that is not so "positive" ask yourself:

- ◆ What good came from this event?
- ◆ Was what happened beyond my control?
- ◆ How will I choose to react to this situation?
- ◆ What have I learned that can help me in the future?
- ◆ Is there any humor in what transpired?
- ◆ What changes can I implement so that this won't happen again?

♦ What can I do in case history repeats itself?
♦ Is there anything I can do to prevent history from repeating itself?

When speaking of things that happen, my friend John Marti and I often say, "There's a story in this somewhere." Then we search to find the story and try to develop it into a format that will hopefully help others who may find themselves in the same or similar circumstances.

During college, my friend Tracy Alan Wood and I were both members of the Alpha Gamma Rho Fraternity. Tracy shared with me the following story:

"It was my second semester of college and I had just finished pledging my fraternity when I met a young lady by the name of Jen. She had asked me to attend a ball given by her sorority on a Saturday night. I was flattered with the invitation and accepted. The following Saturday we attended the ball and had a very good time. I thought I'd made a great impression.

"The following Monday morning, when I came down for breakfast at the fraternity house, several of my fraternity brothers approached me and informed me that I'd received some flowers earlier that morning. Now, not being above receiving flowers from a young lady, I was excited and hurried into our great room, and there on top of the piano were a dozen beautiful red roses. Several of my frat brothers gathered around as I opened the card. My fingers peeled open the envelope and much to my dismay the card read . . . 'Thanks for a great evening! I love you, Butch.'

"Needless to say my friends broke into immediate laughter and word spread quickly around the house of my new relationship.

"I phoned the florist who had delivered the flowers and found that there was a young lady attending the university by the name of Tracy L. Wood and our addresses had been confused. Therefore, I had received her roses.

"The florist apologized and told me to keep the flowers and they would send out another order to Ms. Wood.

"I then went to our local WalMart and purchased a card for my beloved Jen and delivered the flowers to her that very afternoon. The other Tracey received her flowers, my girlfriend received hers, and Butch and I came out smelling like roses."

Making the best of a bad situation can be done by changing our thoughts and frame of mind.

We can choose to control our thoughts or allow our thoughts to control us.

◆ Be careful of your thoughts because they become actions.

- Be careful of your actions because they develop habits.
- Be careful of your habits because they develop character.
- Be careful of your character because it determines destiny.
- Be careful of your destiny, because your destiny will become the legacy you leave.

We must have power over our minds. Throughout our lives we have been rained upon by negative attitudes and negative people. We can become saturated with pessimistic thoughts and drown in self-absorbed pity. We can look at the good side of a situation or choose to concentrate on the bad. Life is not always perfect and we are constantly faced with problems that we must solve. We all suffer losses in life, but it is the person who overcomes these tragedies and makes a success of his or her life who is the winner.

Everyone knows someone who constantly criticizes others and continuously points out the areas in which they fall short. In fact, when we look at the life of a "criticizer", we find that it is in constant turmoil because he or she does not practice what they preach.

When we criticize others, are we critiquing ourselves? When we should clean out our own closets and dust off the shelves.

Instead we try to run everyone else's life and never look at our own.
Instead we create stress and strife in someone else's home.

We should apply our own judgments by looking in the mirror.
We should clean off our glasses to make things clearer.

Should we read our own minds and mind our own lives?
Should we pay more attention to our husbands and wives?

Know that no one likes a bigot invading their house.
Know that no one likes a whiner degrading his or her spouse.

Better mind your own business and work on yourself.
Better know when we criticize others . . . we may be critiquing ourselves.

(Please note the first word in each stanza . . . *WHEN INSTEAD WE SHOULD KNOW BETTER!*)

As parents, spouses, leaders and managers of people, we must live our lives as an example for others to follow. As leaders of people we must apply our own judgment to our own lives and constantly work on getting our own houses in order.

I must emphasize the fact that we can be a positive influence to others, but we cannot change them since change comes from within.

Positive change begins with a great attitude.

- ◆ You show me unhappy parents, and I'll show you unhappy children.
- ◆ You show me unhappy teachers, and I'll show you unhappy students.
- ◆ You show me unhappy managers and I'll show you unhappy associates.
- ◆ You show me motivated, enthusiastic, positive and happy people, and I'll show you a community in which it is a pleasure work, live, and raise our children.

It begins with "An Attitude Adjustment."

INVESTING IN FUTURES

After a presentation, I was visiting with a lady who had one of the most demanding, rewarding, satisfying, trying, and sometimes unappreciated jobs available, that of full-time mother.

As the mother of three children, she strived to teach them right from wrong, responsibility for their actions, morals, values, and the importance of being fiscally responsible. She shared with her children and shared with me what I thought was a rather innovative idea.

She said, from the time that her children could understand finances, money, and its value, she started working on teaching them to be responsible and to realize that money, in fact, "does not grow on trees."

She was completely open and honest about the family budget by including her children in decisions about how the family income would be spent. She told and showed her children exactly what her husband earned monthly by showing them his paycheck stub.

Next, she counted out exactly what he earned (gross pay) in Monopoly money and toy change bought at her local Dollar Store. Together they would lay out all their monthly bills (mortgage, car payment, insurance, electric, natural gas, grocery, automobile fuel, cable television, telephone, credit cards, etc.) and they would pay them together.

First, they would determine, based on the paycheck stub, how much was taken out for Federal Withholding Tax, State Income Tax, Social Security and Medicare. Next they would deduct the amount of these taxes from the Monopoly money and mark it with Post It Notes. The family would then proceed through the stack of bills, taking out funds for each outstanding debt. Upon completion of paying all debts, they would determine their net gain or loss and make additional decisions based upon the balance of their accounts.

(It is amazing that when you count out money for taxes you actually pay or write a check to the Federal and State Government, how conservative you start becoming. I have found that most lawmakers have an overabundance of common sense when it comes to spending our tax dollars. Apparently because they have never used any of it!)

For example, "We have $350.00 worth of disposable income left for the remainder of the month. Gregory wants a new pair of Nike shoes that cost $100.00. If he purchases these, that would leave us with a total of $250.00. Sarah would like to buy a new doll with all the accessories at a

cost of $50.00, leaving us with $200.00. Patrick wants a new Gameboy, which costs $125.00, leaving us $75.00. Sounds okay, right?

"However, each of you have a field trip coming up with your school that will cost you $20.00 apiece for entrance to the theme park, for a total of $60.00, leaving us with $15.00, and that doesn't include food or souvenirs. We want to go to the movies this weekend as a family. Gregory wants to go bowling with his friends next weekend. We are planning a family vacation to Disney World next summer that will cost us $1,200.00, which means we must save $100.00 per month to meet our goal.

"What should we do?"

The children would then start finding ways in which to save money. Maybe Gregory would settle for a less expensive pair of shoes; they would pack a lunch for the theme park; Sarah would decide on a cheaper doll, and Patrick might find that he didn't really need a Gameboy. The youngsters would begin making decisions about how to better meet the financial needs of their family. They would realize that certain decisions had to be made and by having a part in the decision-making process didn't feel as frustrated as they would if the parents said, "No, you can't have that," without explanation as to why. They worked together as a family and everyone felt important.

Teaching our children to be financially sound will be a skill that will help them as they raise their own children.

Our televisions, radios, and newspapers, on a daily basis, are full of offers for easy credit, no money down, don't pay anything for a year, consolidate your bills, take that vacation you have been dreaming of and pay later, and on and on and on.

Credit, especially credit cards, too often are used to provide immediate satisfaction and gratification without much thought to the consequence of running up bills that we cannot repay without forfeiting large amounts of interest. We should use credit as a tool to build our lives when too often it becomes a wrecking ball that wreaks havoc on our finances and is the number one destroyer of marriages. By running up excessive debt, we get caught in a trap that can take years to get out of, if in fact we ever recover.

We should learn the lessons of our grandparents who often emphasize that we should never purchase anything for which we can't afford to pay cash.

Mattel has recently released, for sale, a new Barbie doll that comes with her own miniature unlimited credit MasterCard and a matching realistically sized card for your child. Your child swipes the card through the register and it approves a purchase of $96.00 **every time**.

Is this just another method to brainwash society into spending money without realizing consequences? Is it a plan to begin imprinting upon our children the idea that they can buy anything they want even though they may not be able to afford the items? When they become adults, will they give a moment's thought to repaying those debts? Or will this be a catalyst that destroys their lives and affects their futures in a destructive fashion?

With all the outside influences trying to get us to spend, spend, spend, we must try as parents to offset the trend by teaching our children to be financially independent and fiscally responsible. If we don't teach them, who will?

Growing up in a family of nine (seven children plus two parents), we didn't have "money to burn." My father would budget a certain number of dollars for new shoes, clothes, toys, a bicycle, etc., for each child. If, for example, he planned on spending $25.00 for each child on a bicycle, we had to find a bike that met that budget. He did provide us with the opportunity to buy a more expensive bicycle. His deal, "If you will earn one half of what the more expensive bicycle costs, I will match it." So, if we wanted a $50.00 bike, if we would work and earn $25.00, he would work overtime and match that amount.

What that did was provide us with an incentive to WORK and EARN something extra. On the other hand, we found

that some of the "extras" weren't worth working for and suddenly were not so important. We began to understand the value of hard work and took pride in the goods that we helped to buy. We ultimately took better care of those items than if they had just been given to us. This helped us to develop a work ethic during childhood that carried over into our adult lives.

I remember buying a new pair of shoes, and the excitement and enthusiasm was tremendous. I put my "old worn out" shoes in the box and the new ones on my feet. I knew then that I could run faster, jump higher, and leap farther than any other kid at school. I begged my father to carry me out of the store so I wouldn't get my new shoes dirty. My father said, "Son, I think it's about time you walked out on your own. You're twenty years old."

Sometimes, as parents, we want to "give" our children everything that they desire. That is not necessarily a good thing. Though we want our children to "have it better than we did" showering them with gifts is not always the answer. We can reward our children for outstanding work with a gift or financial incentive, and that can be a tool to encourage positive behavior. Some parents choose to give their children a weekly allowance for good grades and helping out at home.

The first I heard of an "allowance" was in the sixth grade. I discovered that my friend Jim received money from his mom and dad at the end of each week. He did odd jobs at home, studied harder for exams, and pitched in whenever possible. His reward . . . money! I thought this was pretty cool. I approached my dad one afternoon and in a squeaky little voice said, "Dad, Jim gets an allowance from his mom and dad each week for taking out the garbage, doing chores around the house, and for good grades. Dad, can I have an allowance?" My father looked me right in the eye and said, "Patrick, some parents have to pay their children to be good, but I'm so proud of you, you're good for nothing!"

Wow, what a good child I must have been! I was good for nothing! (It was only after graduation from college that I realized, this wasn't a compliment.)

It is important that we find innovative ways to recognize our spouses, children, and associates for jobs well done. But it is equally important that we not put too much emphasis on the idea that more money equates with greater success. Doing well financially does not necessarily mean that your life will be happier and/or healthier. Let's remember . . . we can't take it with us.

It is not the possessions of life that make it worth living, but the quality of the relationships with family and friends that are the true joys.

I continue to be amazed by the ideas people have come up with to teach responsibility to others, especially to children. One man told me of an innovative way by which he and his wife were sending their four children to college. His children were all three and one half to four years apart in age. What they did was this. His oldest daughter wanted to go to college and applied to a major university and was accepted. She then applied for and received several small scholarships and a Pell Grant. They sat down and determined how much her tuition, books, apartment rent, and meals would cost. They subtracted this amount from her scholarships and grant money to determine her outstanding debt for four years of college. The daughter would get a part time job while at school to pay some expenses and have spending money, and her parents would cover the rest.

The mother and father created a college account that the daughter could draw funds from on a monthly basis. Next, the parents drew up a legal contract that the three of them signed. This agreement required that upon graduation from college the daughter would have six months in which to secure a job and begin repaying the college account. The money she repaid would be used to help send the next child to college, then the next, and finally the last. After all four graduated from college, the remaining money would be used to supplement the parent's retirement income.

By implementing this plan the children were more fiscally responsible with the money they spent as they knew that they were obligated to repay the loan. They also took great pride in knowing that they would be helping their

siblings to gain a college education. What a tremendous learning experience that was for all.

At the age of 17, I dented our family car in a minor fender bender. I recall the fear of "What was dad going to do when he found out?" I worried and worried about his response, and when I returned home that evening, I delayed telling about the accident. When the time finally came to tell what happened, I did. Dad's response, "Are you okay?" "Yes," I responded. Dad then said, "Don't worry about the car, it can be fixed. But you cannot be replaced, and you're more valuable than a vehicle." His response was a relief, but more importantly, the value he gave to my life and sense of worthiness was priceless. The lesson: **Never cry over anything that cannot cry over you**!

What children need is parents as role models. The best thing we can spend on children is TIME. A time management survey showed that the average working parent spends less than 30 seconds per day in meaningful conversation with their children. That's 30 seconds beyond small talk. That same child spends hours and hours in front of the television. What they really need is our guidance and open lines of communication. Our children need to know that we are supportive of them, concerned with what is happening in their lives, and available to discuss the obstacles and rewards of life. Children must have rules to live by and realize that there are boundaries and lines that they must not cross. We must enforce those parameters and instill our values and beliefs in our children.

Television and radio talk shows constantly exhibit "young people" out of control. They show children disrespecting one another, their parents, and authority in general. We are expected to believe that this behavior just happened overnight when in most cases it took years to develop.

My family has always had large dogs, not lap dogs but the big ones that will eat you out of house and home. Three rewards I promised myself, upon graduation from college, were a new truck, a bass boat, and a Rottweiler dog (You Might Be a Redneck...). Proudly, I did fulfill all three goals in the above mentioned order. In June of 1986, I bought a Rottweiler named Heidi from a friend of mine, Diana Durrance. Ms. Durrance gave me a bit of advice when I picked this "puppy" up and prepared to take her home. She said, "Never let Heidi do anything as a puppy that you do not want her to do when she's full-grown. For example, if you don't want Heidi to jump on you when she weighs 130 pounds, don't let her jump on you when she weighs 20 pounds. If you don't want the dog to snap at you when it's grown, don't let it snap at you when it's little. Don't let her develop habits as a puppy that you may or may not have to break when she gets older. Give her plenty of discipline, respect, and most importantly love, and she will love you in return."

This policy was implemented and Heidi is one of the sweetest, most gentle and obedient dogs I have ever had.

Although there may not be an exact correlation between the raising of children and the raising of pets, I think that there is a direct relationship when it comes to appropriate behavior and training.

The young people that are out of control on these talk shows may have been out of control as toddlers. For example, did these children talk back to their parents at the age of two and a half and get away with it? Were these children disrespectful to others when they were little? Did they show a total disregard for authority and rules? Chances are the answer is yes. Why, then, should we expect them to change their behavior now that they're older?

Children demand and generally respect authority and discipline. And they will get it whether it's from their parents or our court systems. We must invest in our children while they are in our homes and in our schools instead of having to invest in our penal system later in life. *Life is not a dress rehearsal.* We have but a short period of time in which to instill our values and beliefs in our children, and we must use that time wisely.

By encouraging our children to be involved in extracurricular activities at school and in our communities (clubs, organizations, athletic programs, church, band, chorus, scouts, etc.), we find that they become more civic minded and community responsible.

My brothers and sisters and I were blessed to have parents that were very supportive of all the things we did. My father, on numerous occasions, worked two and three jobs to make ends meet and still, somehow, found time to be involved in our lives. He and my mother attended virtually every activity that we participated in during our years in school and into our adult lives. He often said, "It is much more fun to attend the things your children are doing right than to sit in a courtroom and watch them being incarcerated for doing something wrong."

If we choose to bring a child into this world, we must invest the time and effort to insure that they get a superb start. Get involved in the lives of our children and get involved now, for once tomorrow is here, today and all of its opportunities will be gone forever. Our children make up 25% of our population, but they are 100% of our future.

We must teach our children that they are responsible for their actions and reactions, and we must assist them to make positive choices and decisions.

Everyone is a teacher whether we are in a classroom with students, parents of children, or managers of people in our businesses and organizations. We have the opportunity on a daily basis to train others in order to help them overcome the adversities of life. We must, however, practice the lessons we teach and live by example.

> No written word or mortal plea,
> Can teach young hearts what they should be,
> Nor all the books upon the shelves,
> But what the teachers are themselves.

When a person says, "Do as I say, not as I do," he is a hypocrit. When he says, "Do as I do, not as I did," he is a teacher.

I met a fifth grader who informed me that he was in trouble at home. I inquired as to what happened. He replied, "I forgot to feed the dog." "Is that your job," I asked. "Yes sir, I'm supposed to feed the dog everyday." "Well," I said, "Why didn't you feed the dog?" He said, "After school the other day, my friends came over to my house to play football, and we had a great time. We played until dark, and I went in the house to eat dinner. My dad asked me if I'd fed the dog and I told him I hadn't. He got mad and put me on restriction." I said, "Whose fault was it?" He snapped, "The dog's!"

I told him, "It's not the dog's fault, it's yours! You had a job to do, and you did not do it; therefore, you must face the consequences, which in this case is restriction."

We must give our children and associates responsibility and demand that they live up to that responsibility and

complete tasks and assignments that are given. We seem to live in a time when people around the world will not take responsibility for themselves and want to blame someone else for their problems.

There is an old story about a young boy (I'll call him Matthew), who was in his living room playing with his toy train. When the train pulled into the station, he would say, "All you old codgers getting off of the train, get off, and all you old codgers getting on the train, get on and hurry up." Matthew would then start the train on another trip around the tracks. His mother heard him speaking to the "pretend" passengers in a way that was not acceptable in her home and decided to ease-drop while he continued playing. When the train stopped again, her son said, "All you old coots getting off of the train, get off. All you old coots getting on the train, get on and hurry. We don't have time to wait for you!" Right then, his mother stepped into the living room and said, "Matthew, let me tell you something. Your father and I will not allow you to treat people with that kind of disrespect whether they are real or imaginary. You should not call other people bad names! You should treat them the way you want to be treated. That type of behavior is not permitted in this house, and we expect you to treat others with dignity. I want you to go up to your room for a two-hour time-out. Don't you come back down until you have learned a lesson and can treat others nicely."

Matthew walked down the hall and slowly climbed the stairs to his bedroom. He sat on the edge of his bed and watched the time tick slowly by on his clock. After a grueling two hours he quickly descended the stairs and ran to the kitchen where his mother was preparing dinner. He excitedly exclaimed, "Mommy, two hours is up, can I play with my train?" Matthews' mother said, "Did you learn a lesson?" "Yes, ma'am," he said. "What did you learn, Matthew?" asked his mom. "I learned that we need to treat other people nicely," he said. His mother asked, "Do you think you can play nice and be a good boy?" "Yes," he replied. "Okay, Matthew, you can play with your train."

Matthew ran into the living room and immediately started his train. The train quickly made its way around the tracks and stopped at the station. His mother listened from the other room. Matthew said, "All you nice people getting off of the train, get off, and take your time. All you beautiful people getting on the train, get on and I'll even help you with your luggage. Tickets please, the train is about to leave the station. Last call. All aboard! And if any of you are mad about the two-hour delay . . . take it up with the old bitty in the kitchen!"

(I have amended the language of that joke slightly.)

Like young Matthew, it seems that a large number of people want to blame their problems on someone else. Instead of realizing that we have made a poor decision and working to rectify the predicament we created, we want to "pass the buck" onto someone else. Sadly, it is easier to accuse another of being the cause of our shortfalls than realize that by making poor choices we put ourselves in situations that cause trouble for ourselves and others. Only when we accept the fact that we control our own destiny and quit making excuses for not achieving our goals can we begin building and creating our futures.

It takes a very strong person to admit that he or she made a mistake and to make some good come from that error.

We all have a job to do. That is to prepare ourselves in the best way possible for the future. *We know not what the future holds but we do hold our future.* We are responsible for ourselves and, as parents, for our children. Where we end up tomorrow or twenty years from now depends on the choices we make today. We must continue to educate our minds and work as hard as possible to lay a solid foundation upon which we can build.

No one in this world owes you or me anything! If we want the best out of life, we must earn it. Life is not easy. It takes hard work, dedication, education, good decision-making skills, and the support and encouragement of one another.

As leaders and citizens of the United States, we must respect one another for who we are. Let's take time to get to know our neighbors. If we are in a position in

which we lead others (this includes raising our children), it is imperative that we listen to their thoughts and find out their likes and dislikes, opinions and beliefs. Hearts are beating around us each and every day. True, some hearts are beating to a different drummer; however, it's the "different" beats, tunes, and tones that make beautiful music.

This means that we must open our minds and create our futures. For the decisions we make today will directly impact our lives tomorrow.

We all make choices and decisions on an hourly basis. We make some decisions that too many may seem minor or routine.

For example:

> What time we will rise in the morning?
> What will we eat for breakfast?
> What will we wear to work or school?

During the same day we may have to make major decisions like:

> What direction do we want our businesses to take?
> What goals will we set for the next fiscal year, and who will work on and complete those projects?
> What investments will bring the greatest returns?

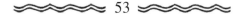

When will I study for final exams?
Should I apply for scholarships and, if so, which
  ones?
What is the best way to lead those who elected
  me?

When the time comes to make both minor and major decisions, try asking yourself some of the following questions:

Is this the right thing to do? Yes or no? If the
  answer is yes, do it. If the answer is no,
  find the right thing to do.
Does this choice support my values and beliefs?
Does this decision show my true character?
Will I be proud of this decision?
Who besides myself will this decision affect?
What are the possible outcomes of this choice?
Will the choice I am about to make benefit me,
  my family or the ones I am leading?

Another set of questions you might use in making correct choices are:

Whom do I admire the most?
Why do I admire this person?
Do I admire this person's character, values, and
  beliefs?
What would he/she do in this situation?

> Call that person and ask questions and their advice.
>
> Listen to the thoughts of parents, teachers, clergy, friends, etc.
>
> Weigh the information you receive and make an educated decision.

Try to imagine situations ahead of time and think about how you would respond. For example, ask yourself the question, "What if . . ."

- ♦ What if a supervisor at work asked me to do something that went against my morals and/or beliefs, what would I do?
- ♦ What if peers were encouraging me to make a destructive choice (alcohol/drinking and driving/drugs/sex/breaking curfew/not studying, etc.)?
- ♦ What if I were asked to compromise my principles on the job?
- ♦ What if I were being pressured to make a choice about a promotion that might harm the welfare of my family?

What would I do? How would I handle this situation? What options do I have?

This can be an effective tool in preparing ourselves for the unexpected.

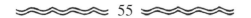

No decision we make during our lives is perfect, and occasionally we will make wrong choices--that's part of life. We have all met individuals during our lives who make some of the same destructive decisions almost daily with the same terrible consequences. That's ignorance.

If we learn from our mistakes, then they become lessons!

Another step is to stand up for what we believe in and take responsibility for our actions. As a country song puts it, "You've got to stand for something or you'll fall for anything."

Our prisons are full of individuals who want to blame "society" for their problems. Some people want to point the finger at everyone except themselves for the poor choices and decisions they make. Many of these individuals have never been held responsible in their entire lives, and their denial becomes a pattern into their adult years. Eventually, society must hold every individual accountable and administer punishment for not maintaining our standards for moral and ethical living.

As we guide and direct our children, we must weigh the importance of the lessons we teach and the punishments we deliver for breaking rules and regulations and going outside of the perimeters we've set.

A gentleman in Arizona told me of one way he cured his children of writing on the walls. If one of his four children

drew on a wall with a crayon or marker, he made him or her clean the wall with soap and a sponge (normal reaction by most parents). With four children he said this was a never-ending battle. One day, he had an idea and decided to implement it. He decided that he would give the children one wall in their basement (playroom) upon which they could write, color, paint and draw with crayons and markers anytime they had the urge to.

When they were toddlers their markings started out as a series of scribbled lines. As the children grew older and entered school, the drawings began to take shape as stick figures and brightly colored scenes. During their teen years the pictures they "doodled" became scenes that really brightened up the room.

Occasionally, he would take a marker and write down a date next to a drawing and the artists' name. Eventually, his children grew up, graduated from high school, married, and started families of their own. The "Doodle" wall is now their favorite place in the entire house. He and his wife often sit in front of the wall and reminisce about the great times they had with their children and reflect upon the many memories they created. He even joked that if they ever move, they are going to take the wall with them.

His solution cured the children from writing on walls in other parts of their home, and, though they never dreamed it at the time, provided them with one of their most prized possessions. They have started their grandchildren's "Doodle" wall.

If we look and think hard enough, we can find ways that, instead of saying don't do this and don't do that, we can provide alternative activities. Instead of just saying no, we can say yes.

I firmly believe that we must continue to reinforce the fact that we love and respect our children. They can never hear those reassuring words too much. My wife Rozanne and I implemented a letter-writing plan for our three children. Throughout each year we write a letter to each child, sharing what they did during that last year, what they've learned, how proud we are of their accomplishments, and how much we love them. The day of their birthday, we each seal the letter we've written, address it to our home and mail it at the local post office. The letter is then postmarked with the day and year. After receiving the letter in the mail, we put it in a small safe we've purchased. We will present the letters to each child on his or her sixteenth birthday.

We wish to reinforce the fact that to us they are the most precious people on the face of this earth. Heaven forbid, but if something should happen to us and we pass away, each child will have a very personal reminder of our love and dedication.

It's the simple little things in life that can make a tremendous difference! What is the least expensive thing we can do for our children that will be the greatest investment in their lives? Spend time with them! Children deserve to be parented, and it is our responsibility to meet that obligation.

Statistics show that as many as seven out of ten children between the ages of 10 and 14 go home to an empty house at the end of the school day. That means that 70% of our children are unsupervised. It is my opinion that we have lost our focus and have our priorities scrambled. Juvenile crime has increased dramatically in our communities, and most of that crime takes place prior to parents returning home from work. Discipline problems and violence continue to increase in our schools (if we would discipline our children, emphasize the importance of education and support the teachers, they could teach). Teen pregnancy is on a continual rise. Most teenage girls become pregnant between the hours of 3:00 and 5:00 in the afternoon. Drug and alcohol abuse among teens is steadily increasing. This increase in promiscuous behavior is due to a lack of supervision and guidance.

We may be trying too hard to keep up with the neighbors. The result is that our children are suffering. (*It used to be that parents sacrificed so their children could have it better. Now parents are sacrificing their children so they might have more possessions.*)

I am reminded of the song by Harry Chapin entitled, "Cat's in the Cradle." I think there is a strong message in the lyrics for all of us.

My child arrived just the other day,
He came to the world in the usual way.
But there were planes to catch, and bills to pay.
He learned to walk while I was away.
And he was talking 'fore I knew it, and as he grew,
He'd say, "I'm gonna be like you, dad.
You know I'm gonna be like you."

And the cat's in the cradle and the silver spoon,
Little boy blue and the man in the moon.
"When you coming home, dad?" "I don't know when,
But we'll get together then.
You know we'll have a good time then."

My son turned ten just the other day.
He said, "Thanks for the ball, dad, come on let's play.
Can you teach me to throw?" I said, "Not today,
I got a lot to do." He said, "That's ok."
And he walked away, but his smile, lemme tell you,
Said, "I'm gonna be like him, yeah.
You know I'm gonna be like him."

And the cat's in the cradle and the silver spoon,
Little boy blue and the man in the moon.
"When you coming home, dad?" "I don't know when,

But we'll get together then.
You know we'll have a good time then."

Well, he came from college just the other day,
So much like a man I just had to say,
"Son, I'm proud of you. Can you sit for a while?"
He shook his head, and he said with a smile,
"What I'd really like, dad, is to borrow the car keys.
See you later. Can I have them please?"

And the cat's in the cradle and the silver spoon,
Little boy blue and the man in the moon.
"When you coming home, son?" "I don't know when,
But we'll get together then, dad.
You know we'll have a good time then."

I've long since retired and my son's moved away.
I called him up just the other day.
I said, "I'd like to see you if you don't mind."
He said, "I'd love to, dad, if I could find the time.
You see, my new job's a hassle, and the kid's got the flu,
But it's sure nice talking to you, dad.
It's been sure nice talking to you."
And as I hung up the phone, it occurred to me,
He'd grown up just like me.
My boy was just like me.

And the cat's in the cradle and the silver spoon,
Little boy blue and the man in the moon.
"When you coming home, son?" "I don't know when,

But we'll get together then, dad.
You know we'll have a good time then."

by Harry Chapin (lyrics by Sandra Chapin).
Description: Originally found on album Verities &
    Balderdash. Also found on Greatest Stories Live,
    1975; Anthology of Harry Chapin, 1985; the Gold
    Medal Collection, 1988; and the Bottom Line Encore
    Series, 1998.

We have only one chance to raise our children. We must
invest in futures on a daily basis, not financial futures
that will return us more money, but in the futures of our
children, the futures that can pay the greatest dividends
of all. When we realize the contributions we've made to
their lives, and the ultimate return on our investment of
time, patience, education and love as we look into the
eyes of the next generation will be worth the effort. Our
children are our greatest natural resource.

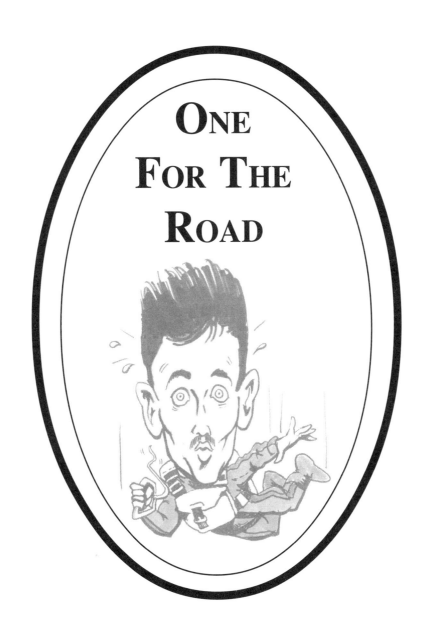

ONE
FOR THE
ROAD

ONE FOR THE ROAD

O ne of the single biggest influences on adults *and* young people is the impact our friends and peers have upon our lives. Often we do things we think will make us "fit in" and to be part of the "with it" crowd in order to be seen favorably by our peers. We buy designer jeans, designer shirts, designer sweaters, designer shoes, designer socks and, yes, even designer underwear. Some take up smoking, drinking, and even premarital sex just so they won't be considered "uncool" or be looked down upon by those whose admiration they seek. At one time or another we've all done something we wouldn't normally do because of the encouragement of others.

Back in 1980 a group of friends and I were attending a conference in Orlando, Florida. As we drove down Orange-Blossom Trail heading to our final destination, we had the car stereo blaring louder than the engine roar of a Boeing 757. We were excited to be "out on our own" for the weekend and allowed our enthusiasm get us a little carried away. We stopped at a red light, and one of the occupants of the vehicle yelled, "Fire Drill!" Almost immediately, we swung all four doors open, jumped from the car, and ran in circles around it screaming as loudly as we could. Just as the light turned green, we jumped back into the car, slammed the doors shut, and "mashed the gas."

Suddenly, from out of nowhere blue lights began flashing. It was as though we had entered a disco. Upon looking in the rear view mirror we noticed the source of the light. Right on our bumper was one of Orlando's finest men in blue. Yes, the bubble gum machine had hit the jackpot. As we pulled over and stopped the car, Mr. Policeman, crab walk and all, approached our vehicle and asked for identification from the entire group. He asked, "Do you know why I pulled you over?" My reply, as if I didn't have a clue, "No, sir." He said, "It's because of that little stunt all of you pulled back there at the intersection." Feeling my oats, I replied, "Were we running too fast?" That was apparently the wrong thing to say to an underpaid, overtired police officer who didn't feel like dealing with a group of rowdy, out-of-town teenagers who felt invincible.

The sermon began. He proceeded to share with us why what we had done was dangerous not only to ourselves but other drivers. How we could have been seriously injured or killed because of our juvenile stunt. After his powerful presentation, he was kind enough to let us off with only a warning.

Now, do you think that if I were driving down the road by myself, I would, on the spur of the moment have dreamed about jumping out the car and chasing myself around it? Probably not. But our overzealous attitudes and the pressure of trying to fit in and impress friends overcame our common sense. (I only wish this were the dumbest thing I've ever done.)

We've all been in situations where we didn't use the best judgment and in some instances paid a much greater price than a lawman's warning.

Sadly, a number of individuals are never able to resist the inclination to do "inappropriate" things to impress others. Because some people never grow up, we must instill in our children the desire to do good things that have positive results rather than to give in to childish pranks that may eventually lead to a life of uncertainty. Again, I will emphasize the importance of leading by example and encouraging others to do great things. It is better to have one friend that encourages us to do the right thing and have them praise you when you succeed than to have ten so-called "friends" that belittle your accomplishments. You consciously choose who your friends will be. You also choose your destiny, and no one else can decide how successful you will be in the game of life.

My grandfather used to call me, "Running Bear." He called me Running Bear when I ran around naked. "Running Bear, you're the only one who can decide where you're going in life and who your friends are. Let me tell you a secret. You are going to turn out like the people you hang around with. If you want to be successful, hang around with successful people. If you want to be a dud, hang around with duds!"

Words of wisdom, from a very wise man. "If you want to be successful, hang around with successful people!" The people we choose as friends have a direct influence on how we think, act, and react. Our friends can be assets as we work our way to the top or liabilities on the climb.

Look around! A majority of the time we find that drug addicts hang around with drug addicts! Alcoholics associate with alcoholics! High school dropouts select other dropouts as friends. This is not true in every case, but we find that these individuals cling to one another. Why? Peer pressure--the single greatest force in the lives of many individuals. Sometimes we make decisions, not because of what we believe in our hearts, but based on what we want others to think of us.

Ricky was an average high school student who as a ninth grader started a part-time job, working for a friend virtually every weekend. As a tenth grader he began working after school as well. By the time Ricky was a junior in high school, he was working weekends, after school, and late into the evenings. During his senior year his hard work and dedication really began to pay off. He drove one of the nicest cars in the high school parking lot, wore the sharpest clothes on campus and was looked up to and admired by a large number of his classmates. The point? Although his commitment to his work was admirable, Ricky was killed on the job. He was killed when the bullet from a rival drug dealer struck him down. He had paid the ultimate price for choosing an occupation that brought with it certain risks to himself personally and tremendous damage to the lives of his "customers." He had made the wrong choice.

Sure, he had the drive and determination to succeed, but he made a very poor choice of friends and occupations.

Sadly, this story is typical of virtually every community throughout the United States. The incredible thing is that in many cases such thugs are the ones that some young people look up to as role models. They see these people as heroes and give them complimentary names like "street pharmacist." These drug dealers look at abusing the minds and bodies of others by hooking them on drugs and then supplying their habit as an easy way to make quick money.

Peer pressure is a powerful force. One of the top reasons people join gangs is peer pressure and the positive recognition they receive from their fellow gang bangers for doing something wrong. Ninety percent of high school dropouts have two things in common. One, they are hooked on drugs or alcohol, and two, they are *not* involved in any extracurricular activities. They are not involved in the band, the chorus, clubs or organizations, or athletic

programs. They don't have a sense of belonging. We must encourage our children to get involved in school. To support them and emphasize the many opportunities beyond the academics of classroom.

Worse, children today face a completely different set of pressures than their parents and grandparents did when they were growing up.

A survey in the 1940's revealed that the top seven problems in public schools then were:

1) talking out of turn
2) chewing gum
3) making noise
4) running in the halls
5) cutting in line
6) violating the dress code
7) littering

In the 90's that list of problems had changed to:

1) drug abuse
2) alcohol abuse
3) pregnancy
4) rape
5) suicide
6) robbery
7) assault

Confronted with these alarming problems, children in every neighborhood throughout America need to learn the difference between right and wrong. The question is: Who will teach values to our kids and whose values will they teach? Studies have shown that one third of all children have lied to their best friends, one half have stolen something, and three quarters have cheated in school. These are daily occurrences. Since 1950, murder by teenagers has increased 232%. It is estimated that during 1998 two and one half million American teenagers will be arrested, and many of them will end up in a juvenile prison. Who are these kids? They are our neighbors, our nieces and nephews, our classmates and, though some of us would not like to admit it, our children. Crimes are not exclusively committed by young men. For every four boys, one girl is arrested. The number of offenses committed by girls is on the rise in almost every community. It's no longer "boys being boys."

We must get back to teaching young people basic moral values and the difference between right and wrong. We must teach them basic caring and decency. We cannot assume that our children already know good values. Doing right or wrong is not an inherited trait, it must be learned. Just as racial hatred and violence are learned traits, so is goodness. Who's job is this? Some people say that "society" must step in and take charge. I beg to differ. Any parent who chooses to bring a child into this world must be held responsible for teaching that child what is acceptable and what is not. We must teach un-provocative, old fashioned decency.

A time management study showed that the average working parents now spends less than thirty seconds per day in meaningful conversation with their kids. That's thirty seconds beyond small talk. During that same day the average child may spend as much as five hours in front of their televisions. Yet we all know that most television shows are not going to help end moral illiteracy, and in many cases T.V. only advances the problem.

Every year, children spend more time in front of their televisions than they do in their classrooms or with their parents. Some kids spend entire days watching music videos, and for some of them the glowing images on the screen are their only heroes. Young people desperately need positive role models to admire. As parents we must set an example and show them that it's good to be good. There does not seem to be as many "good guy" images as there used to be and parents are having to look much harder for worthwhile entertainment for their children.

Together we need to help our children celebrate their accomplishments and bring positive recognition to the things they do that are good. It's our job to build self esteem in the young people whose lives we touch. We must make a conscious effort to try not to do to them some of the same negative things that are occurring out in our neighborhoods. It's very easy to criticize and point out an individual's bad points, but it takes a special person to recognize and reward potential.

Let us not forget: Young people make up approximately 25% of our population but are 100% of our future.

Some of the pressures to experiment with drugs and alcohol first begin in our middle schools and high schools. Of the kids who use drugs, the average age that experimentation begins is now 12 ½ years old. We are occasionally encouraged by our classmates to do things we would not normally do, and we must work on character development to overcome these pressures.

Do you recall your senior year in high school? I can remember much of my twelfth grade year as if it were yesterday (maybe because I spent three years of my life in the twelfth grade . . . not really, but it's a great joke). As seniors we weren't worried about getting to bed early so we wouldn't be tired for school the next day. We weren't very concerned with studying hard for final exams. Our main concern . . . to party!

I grew up in a very small town that had none of the "big city" attractions. We had to create our own excitement. On a typical weekend evening we would go out to a place called "Moccasin Slough." The reason we went out to the "slough" was because our parents couldn't find it, and our police officer couldn't get there. We could party down and have the time of our lives.

Some people would drive their pickup trucks around the swamp, mud slinging. Others would build big camp fires, and still others would have in the trunks of their cars and the beds of their trucks, ice. In that ice, beer!

On one particular Saturday night we were graced by the presence of our friend "Big" John. The reason we called him "Big" John is because he stood about six feet five inches tall, weighed over 250 pounds, and wore shoes so large some of us could have lived in them. John was someone most of us literally looked up to.

John was not much of a beer drinker, but this night, we decided he would be. Someone handed him a beer, and a group gathered around as he gulped his way to the bottom of the first can. When he finished, everyone cheered and pushed another beer towards him. He drank it. After a while he started to feel a little bit "tipsy." John wasn't the most coordinated person in the world anyway, and now that he was slightly drunk, he was quite a sight to see.

John began dancing and singing. He couldn't dance, and his attempt at singing left a great deal to be desired. He was belching, slurring his words, cracking jokes and truly making himself the life of the party. Our laughter could be heard for what seemed like miles through the woods, and John was certainly the main attraction.

"Drink another, drink another!" we shouted. We couldn't wait for school to start the following Monday so we could brag about how much he had been drinking. In retrospect, we probably looked like a group of cheerleaders!

"Big" John drove a totally refurbished, absolutely gorgeous, classic 1957 Chevy. As the party began to wind to a close that night, John was still dancing to music coming from a truck radio. He climbed into his '57 Chevy and was singing to his radio . . . and he didn't even have one!

He left the party followed by several vehicles full of his classmates. There was no way any of the drivers could keep up with John's car, and before long he was out of sight. We did catch up with him a few minutes later. He had stopped in the middle of the road. When we came around the corner, there sat his car right in front of us. He hadn't stopped voluntarily. He'd hit a car load of people head on, killing all the occupants of the other vehicle immediately. But John wasn't dead. When we arrived on the scene of that crash, he was trapped in his 1957 Chevrolet, and the same people who twenty minutes earlier had chanted, "Go John go, drink another," stood there terrified and helpless as his car burst into flames and we listened to him scream in pain as he burned to death inside that automobile.

That truly happened on the Saturday night before our senior class Baccalaureate exercise. Instead of it being the happy, joyous occasion it was supposed to be, we sat there with tears running down our faces because we knew in some small way, each of us had played a part in John's death.

On Tuesday morning instead of going to graduation practice, we went to the cemetery and watched a friend be buried. Not just a friend from our senior year but someone with whom many of his classmates had gone to elementary school, middle school, and high school.

On that ill-fated Saturday night, who could have made a difference? I could. Anyone at that party could have stood up and done the right thing. Someone could have taken his car keys away, stepped in and said, "That's enough." But instead, we chose to go along with the crowd. Whose job is it to step in and watch out for our family and friends? It's yours and mine. Perhaps if one of us, on that dreaded evening, had stood up and done the right thing, "Big" John would be alive today raising his own children.

Granted, no one put a gun to his head and forced him to drink the beer, but through our constant encouragement to do something that our parents, our churches, and our teachers had told us was the wrong thing to do, we encouraged it. Our peer pressure was a powerful weapon that proved to be extremely destructive to families and friends.

Perhaps you can say, "I don't drink, so nothing like that could ever happen to me." But you or someone you love could be the sober, innocent victim in the other automobile. Some people say that a tragedy such as "Big" John's has very little to do with us or our loved ones. However, the impact of such an event can ripple through entire generations.

My grandfather, Benjamin Shaw, is 99 years old. Had he been killed by a drunk driver or an individual under the influence of mind-altering drugs or had he destroyed his life as a teenager by making poor or destructive decisions, would that have anything to do with me? Some people would answer, "No, he's 99 years old that would have happened more than 63 years before you were born and would have no effect upon you." However, it would have directly affected me. My mother and I recently figured out that had my grandfather's (her father) life ended as a teenager, fifty-one people would not be in this world today. Those fifty-one include my mother and her brother and sister, my brothers and sisters and cousins, my precious children and my nieces and nephews, all direct descendants of my grandfather. Those fifty individuals don't even take into consideration the next generation or generations to come. So as you can plainly see, the choices we make today truly impact our tomorrows.

In the United States of America we have millions of drivers on our roads. We need to start telling them that they've got to take more responsibility. You can't just blame crashes like "Big" John's on someone else. We as drivers must be more accountable. Cars have been made safer over the years, and I don't know anyone in the car business or who drives a vehicle who doesn't believe that they can be made even safer. But again the responsibility for increased safety must remain in the hands of the driver. When we talk about security behind the wheel, we must not forget this fact: Over one half of all fatal accidents on the streets and highways of America are alcohol related. In one sweep we could reduce the number of fatal crashes if we took the drunks off of the road and kept them off.

We have to tighten our belts in America. We need to get back to some basic things . . . some character. We must discuss with our children the dangers of poor decision making. We must make them aware of the dangers of drugs and alcohol. We must talk openly about controlling peer pressure and not allowing it to control us. We cannot assume that our schools will address these issues or that our children will automatically know how to combat these pressures. It is never too early to begin addressing such concerns as alcohol, drugs, abstinence and good decision making. Many of the issues we discuss today *will* be the challenges of our tomorrows.

FROM THE MOUTHS OF BABES

FROM THE
MOUTHS OF BABES

After delivering a keynote address to a group of educators attending a conference, I had the opportunity of visiting with one of the delegates, a kindergarten teacher. As most speakers will agree, one of the joys and highlights of any program is the time spent with the tremendous people present and discovering the positive differences they are making in the lives of others.

Now, just about everyone, no matter how old he or she is, can remember their kindergarten or first grade teacher. These individuals have a special rapport with their students and an everlasting impact upon their lives.

Mrs. Johnson had been working with children for many years and loved her work immensely, and she told me the following story:

"One Friday afternoon a teacher's aide entered my classroom and informed me that I had a phone call in the main office. I asked her to take a message as this was Friday, and it was important for me to wrap up my lesson and tell the children good-bye for the weekend. The aide informed me that this was a very important call and that she was sent to cover my class. I was somewhat aggravated and went down to the office to receive the call. On the other end of the line was my sister. She was upset and very emotional, and she informed me that our mother had passed away. This was very unexpected since my mother had never been sick and two nights ago I spoke with her and she said she was feeling wonderful.

"I was devastated. After hanging up, I phoned my husband. He left work immediately and picked me up from school. I even left my car in the parking lot. We went home, packed a few things, and left for the airport to take the very first flight to my mother's hometown.

"As a family, we made final arrangements for her burial, settled family matters, and laid my mother to rest. I cannot begin to describe the pain and anguish I felt from losing my mother and the depression that followed. It seemed that not only had I lost my mother but also a large part of myself. I went through a wide range of emotions from pain to anger and self-pity.

"Two weeks later I returned to the classroom and to my students, but did not realize that I had not fully recovered from the shock and grief of losing my mother. Nor did I understand how much I had changed in such a short period of time.

"At the end of my first week back in the classroom, one little girl asked me, 'Mrs. Johnson, what's wrong?' I replied, 'What do you mean?' She said, 'You aren't like you were before you went on vacation.'

"I said, 'Well, you know how you love your mommy?' The little girl replied, 'I love my mommy very much.' I said, 'My mommy just passed away and is in heaven, and I have been very sad.'

"The young girl replied, 'Did your mommy live until she died?'

"I smiled and said, 'Why, of course she did, honey.'

"With that the child said, 'Mrs. Johnson, you need to live until you die!"

You need to live until you die.

From the mouths of babes comes the wisdom of the ages.

Mrs. Johnson told me that the words from her young student really made her think and reflect on her life. She said she began to appreciate the touching memories she had of her mother and to evaluate how she chose to live her life. She decided also that we need to live until we die, to live life to its fullest; that life is too short to be bitter and pessimistic. We must strive to look for the best in ourselves and others. Treasure our family and friends and cherish both the personal and professional relationships we develop over the years. For we never know when we may lose a special friend or a loved one.

We all suffer losses in life, whether personal or professional, and it is the person who overcomes those losses and makes a success of his/her life, who is the winner.

Several years ago after a presentation to a group of business people the opportunity arose to visit with a number of those in attendance. A group of us sat and talked about the importance of motivating ourselves and our associates and shared ideas of how to maintain enthusiasm in the workplace.

One gentleman said to the rest of us, "You know, I just don't have the fire for my job that I had in the past. I feel burned out. It's a chore to get up each morning and head to work and a joy when 5:00 arrives and I can get out of the building. I guess I'm just burned out."

That individual participated in the conversation for several more minutes as we concentrated our conversation on ways to build a new enthusiasm for our jobs, and then he left.

As soon as he walked away, one of the managers laughed and said, "You know that man being burned out is kind of funny." "What's so funny about being burned out?"

another person asked. The first one went on, "I have worked with that individual since he started with our company over fifteen years ago and he can't be burned out. He was never on fire in the first place!"

You've got to be on fire for the work you are doing before you can be burned out.

Life is too short to be miserable in the work that we do. If a person does not enjoy their chosen occupation, he or she should pursue what they would like to do for a living with an unbridled passion and do it.

Occasionally we all meet individuals who have chosen a career that they despise. My wife and I have a friend who was an excellent high school teacher. He chose to stop teaching and pursue a degree in law. He graduated from law school and secured a job only to find that he hated the practice of law and missed teaching. However, he was so in debt to student loans that he had to continue practicing law in order to pay his bills. He was stuck in a career he did not like. But he refused to allow himself to remain in this situation for the rest of his life and he made the best of a bad situation! He is currently teaching law at Temple University and thoroughly enjoys his work.

My challenge to you is this . . . no matter what age you are. If you have a desire to pursue an occupation other than the one you are presently in, find a part-time job doing what you love to do. If you cannot find a paid position, find someone in that career and volunteer your time. Discover whether you thoroughly enjoy this work and imagine getting paid to do what you love.

Thousands of people, certainly millions, worldwide are stuck in careers that they hate. Don't be one of them.

As parents, managers of people, and educators, we are not responsible for the whole world, but we are responsible first and foremost for ourselves and our families. We have in our country too many people who say there is a social answer for every individual problem and that the reason people don't succeed is because of their environment, because of their surroundings. Some say that because of some environmental factor, a parent, sibling, spouse or child cannot reach their goals. Too many people say that it is not their fault, that they can't help where they are in life. Many say that life dealt them a bad hand.

What they don't say is that we control our own hands. We must play the hand we are dealt to the best of our ability to maximize our chances at success. We are in charge of our own destinies. It doesn't matter where you live. It makes no difference whether you are from a good neighborhood or a bad one (the obstacles may be different, but they can still be overcome). You are responsible for where you end up.

Our jails are full of rich people from great neighborhoods and loving families. Our jails are full of people who had more opportunity than most of us ever dream of having but because of the choices *they* made they are where they are. Those people chose not to exercise their potential and elected to make poor decisions.

As adults and children we sometimes allow ourselves to get into a frame of mind where we think, *my* dad was an alcoholic, which means I'll be an alcoholic. *My* mom's hooked on prescription drugs, that means I'll be hooked on prescription drugs. *My* sister dropped out of high school, that means I'll drop out of high school. *My* brother is in jail, that means I'm going to jail. However, this is far from true because each of us is an individual with control over our destiny.

We must set the standards by which we choose to live our lives. We will make mistakes and sometimes not maintain those standards. However, if we meet and even exceed those standards on a daily basis, perhaps they are not high enough. In those instances, raise the expectations. We do not need to raise them so high that we must be superheroes, but we should all strive to possess heroic qualities.

History books are full of individuals from poor families and less-than-perfect backgrounds that have become great examples of how we can all succeed by maintaining a strong moral character and by working hard.

A few of these people include:

Wilma Rudolph - 1960 Olympic Gold Medalist in Track and Field.
Dave Thomas - founder of Wendy's Restaurants.
Les Brown - motivational speaker and television talk show host.
Oksana Baiul - 1994 Olympic Gold Medalist Figure Skater.
Colonel Harland Sanders - founder of Kentucky Fried Chicken.
Walt Disney – founder and creator of Disney attractions worldwide.
Charles Schultz - creator of Charlie Brown.

What do these individuals have in common? They didn't waste their time trying to level the playing field. They chose instead to focus on their dreams, educate their minds, make choices that complemented their dreams, learn from their mistakes, and make tremendous successes of their lives. They CHANGED their circumstances and rose above their adversity.

They are all ordinary people who chose to be extraordinary.

Each of the above mentioned people have many qualities that you and I possess. We must choose to utilize our best traits.

In the classic movie *The Wizard of Oz*, the Tin Man wanted a heart, the Lion needed courage, the Scarecrow was in search of a brain full of knowledge, and Dorothy wanted to go home. We found at the end of this tale that the Wizard didn't give the Tin Man, Lion, Scarecrow or Dorothy anything they didn't already have. They possessed the qualities they sought but never realized it until it was pointed out to each of them. Why? Because everything they asked for and desired was already inside of them.

Many of us are the same way. We tend to compare ourselves to someone else. We wish we were more like him or more like her. We wish we had his/her skills and abilities when deep down inside we do have their skills and perhaps others that we have never utilized.

Remember: You are the only one who walks the way you do, talks the way you do, thinks the way you do, looks the way you do, looks at life through your eyes--you are unique.

A few years ago I heard the story of a Christmas play put on by a group of mentally handicapped students. The play took place one evening, and as people arrived at the auditorium they came with mixed emotions, not knowing quite what they were in for. Programs were passed out explaining what was about to take place. Actors in the play ranged from the mentally handicapped to a thirty-five year old woman with Downs Syndrome who was to play the part of God.

The audience settled in, the house lights dimmed, spotlights began flashing wildly around the room, and the curtains went up. On the stage stood a cast of characters that ranged from clouds to hills and trees. In the center of the stage, the Almighty God.

The plot was simple. Each character explained how like each of us they had a special ability. The clouds created rain for the plants and animals. The trees and plants provided food and beauty. The rising sun shed light and warmth upon the earth and all her inhabitants.

During the intermission the audience was informed that they would have the opportunity to ask God any question they wanted. Now was a chance! A chance to put God on the spot. To ask why everything they had prayed for was not given to each of them. Why all their prayers had apparently not been answered.

Suddenly, a sharply dressed person stood up in the middle of the auditorium, looked God right in the eye and said, "God, I have prayed to you almost every night. I've asked you to make me happy, make me successful, and give me all those things I want so badly. God, why have you not answered my prayers?"

Silence fell upon the audience. How would I answer a question like that? What would your response be? How would a thirty-five year old woman with Downs Syndrome answer that question? Then God spoke and said, "I made the sun rise, the oceans blue and the grass green. There are some things you must do on your own!"

I made the sun rise, the oceans blue, and the grass green. There are some things we must do on our own.

We can wish, dream, hope, and pray, but if we are unwilling to work and work hard, all our goals and dreams will ever be are fantasies. From this day forward I challenge you to *make* the dream that you dream be the future you reach.

THE QUESTION IS...

Miscommunication! A major cause of divorce, workplace stress, family disagreements, domestic violence, trials and tribulation. It is amazing with the modern technology that includes cordless phones, cell phones, digital phones, video phones, internet chat-rooms, numeric pagers, alphanumeric pagers and fax machines, how little we really talk to one another. We may have lost the art of sitting and talking. Very few homes are built with the large walk-around porches similar to those that our ancestors used to sit upon each evening and discuss a variety of topics. We now spend more time in front of our televisions and computers than with our families. You and I both know people who spend more time in Internet chat-rooms talking to strangers than they spend visiting with their own spouses and children.

No matter how hard we try, however, miscommunication happens in both our personal and professional lives. I heard a story about a little boy who was sitting on the curb with a rather large dog lying at his feet. A man walked up and said, "Son, does your dog bite?" The boy replied, "No sir." The man bent down and attempted to pet the dog when suddenly it jumped at him and bit his hand so hard it drew some blood. The man was furious, he said, "I thought you said that your dog doesn't bite. How do you explain what just happened?" The boy said, "It's easy, this is not my dog."

In another example of miscommunication, a man walked into a pharmacy and asked the pharmacist if he had a cure for the hiccups. The pharmacist said, "Yes" and quickly walked from behind the counter. He approached the man and in a flash hit him so hard right on the nose that it knocked the customer down. Clutching his nose, the customer jumped up and screamed, "What did you do that for?!" The pharmacist replied, "You don't have the hiccups anymore, do you?" The man replied, "No, I never did. My wife out in the car does."

In both instances, it seems at first that a clear message was sent. However, each participant in both conversations was communicating on a different level. The initial speaker was trying to convey a message, and the listener interpreted the message incorrectly.

Though at times we try to be very clear in the things we say or directions we give, we must understand that there can be a great deal of room for interpretation. You and I may hear and understand a question in two different ways just as the participants in the above stories.

The same is true whether the communication is verbal or written. As we pursue our personal and professional goals, we must make sure that we have mapped out a plan that takes into consideration as many details as possible. Several years ago I heard a commercial on the radio that started off with the following: *If we are to ride on the wings of progress, rocketing with confidence through a world of uncertainty, we've got to get this train on track to ensure smooth sailing.* If the objective of the commercial was to confuse the audience with a brief statement to get their attention, it worked. So the question is, did this method of communication work? In fact it did. (The sad thing is that we all know people who talk like this in real life and it can be terribly confusing.) However, mixed metaphors can be helpful tools in making points and communicating messages. It is important to clearly explain the message you are trying to convey with the metaphor to insure that it is understood.

In the State of Florida where I was born and raised, one of the most famous places individuals go to purchase adult beverages (alcohol) is the ABC Liquor Store. These institutions are also popular in both North and South Carolina as well as numerous states throughout the nation. It is not uncommon to see a large number of cars in the parking lot of an ABC Liquor Store and lounges with people rushing around, making purchases and working on their next hangover.

A majority of those purchasing alcohol take it home and consume it within the walls of their houses. However, there is a certain percentage of individuals that choose to drink alcoholic beverages and then get behind the wheels of their automobiles. Their irresponsibility can bring not only terrible physical pain to their bodies and the bodies of others but also wreak havoc upon families worldwide. It is a challenge for law enforcement officers to get these law breakers off of the road.

Dan, a police officer friend of mine was patrolling the streets of Gainesville, Florida, late one Saturday night when he noticed a vehicle weaving down the highway with a driver who was apparently impaired. He turned on his flashing lights and proceeded to pull the vehicle over into the parking lot of a large shopping center. After the car came to a stop, the officer approached the driver and asked him for identification and to step out of his vehicle. Following several minutes of fumbling through his wallet, the driver finally located his license and presented it to the officer. Now it was time for the sobriety test.

The officer asked the driver to close his eyes, tilt his head back, extend his arms, and touch his nose with the tip of his right index finger. The driver's next challenge was to walk a straight line. The final test was one that involved verbal communication. My friend asked the driver to stand with his feet together, tilt his head back, close his eyes and tell him his ABC's. The driver did exactly as instructed and said, "My ABC's. There is one on 34th Street, one on Highway 441, one on Archer Road...." He was immediately handcuffed, placed in the back of the patrol car and taken to the Alachua County Jail. Another victory for the good guys.

In a sad, yet humorous way this is yet another example of two people communicating on a different level. The officer was very specific with his instructions, but the drunk heard something totally different. As we delegate responsibility to our co-workers, students, or children, again we must talk and double check to insure we are understood. We must really listen to what others are saying and make a conscious effort to fully comprehend the ideas we are trying to convey to one another.

Occasionally, we have disagreements, whether with a co-worker, manager, date, spouse, friend, or family member. That is part of life. But we must concentrate on solutions to those misunderstandings instead of compounding the problem by blowing them out of proportion.

Think back to when you first started dating. Remember how you talked a great deal in an effort to get to know one another? Remember that first disagreement? You spent several hours on the telephone trying to patch things up. We've all done it. You stretched every kink out of the phone cord (pre-cordless phones) and locked yourself in the bathroom, your bedroom, or even the pantry in search of privacy from your family or friends. The phone call went something like this. "No, you say it. No, you say it . . . I always have to say it first. . . I love you too! I do miss you very, very much!

"Okay, you're right, I'm wrong! No, I never said you were fat . . .No, I never said you were fat . . . Everybody exercises! You're perfect just the way you are. You're a natural beauty. You're an Ivory Girl. You could get out of bed and go straight to the mall. No, I didn't say you were fat . . . I said you were short for your weight!

"I love you just the way you are. I'm glad we settled that. Okay, I've got to go now. No, you hang up first. No, I always have to hang up first. Okay, let's hang up together. On three, ready? One, two, three . . . are you there? Okay, I'm sorry, I just wanted to see if you would hang up. We'd better go. I love you too. Good night! Okay on three . . . 1, 2, 3! (Click)

(1, 2, 3, 4, 5 . . . RING!) "Hello! Yeah, its me. Of course I still miss you. I've been thinking about you every second, even though it's only been five seconds since I talked to you last. I am glad you called back. Okay, I wanted to hear your voice again, too. We'd better go. I love you, too. Good night . . . are you there? Let's hang up together. Bye!"

Some of you reading this book are saying to yourself, "Patrick, that's silly!" (Which is a funny thing to say to yourself since your name probably isn't Patrick.) Chances are, you've done this. I've done it, we've all done it! What did we do? We communicated. We settled our differences by doing one of the least expensive things we can do and that is talking. When we show a genuine interest in others, listen to what they are saying and make the effort to solve challenges, we can.

Occasionally, we make the wrong decisions. Even when it came to the people we dated. Sometimes we found that the girl or guy we had a tremendous crush on actually turned out much different than we expected.

Guys, do you remember the first time you asked out that special someone? You finally got up the nerve to ask her out. You walked up and with all the confidence you could muster in your most suave and debonair fashion said, Aummmmmm . . . uhhhhhhhhh . . . would you . . . mmmmmmmmm . . . go out with me? Low and behold she said, "Yes."

You agreed on the next Friday night. Now, prior to your date, you ran home, cleaned your car inside and out, took a shower, shaved your peach fuzz, put on a half can of deodorant and three quarters of a bottle of cologne. (Let's face it, guys, we were in the bathroom and looked like we were warming up for the starring role in a Karate Kid movie.) Then you walked down the hallway to the master bedroom and stood in front of the life-sized mirror and did those JC Penny poses. We knew there was no one "cooler" than the stud looking back at us.

WHO PACKS THE PARACHUTE?

In order to make a great impression, you arrived at your date's house fifteen minutes early. You rang the doorbell and the biggest, meanest, ugliest, most intimidating man you ever saw in your life opened the door. There stood her father, towering over you and checking you out from head to toe. He invited you in, told you to have a seat on the couch, and informed you that his daughter would be ready in a few minutes.

By the time you reach the couch you are questioning whether this date is a good idea or not. You start feeling warm. Beads of perspiration gather on your forehead. You think the walls are closing in on you. You feel as though you are sinking into the cushions of the couch and almost wish the sofa would open up and swallow you. A giant lump forms in your throat. Then her father speaks. "So, where are you two off to this evening?" Your mind races and you reply, "Well . . . first, I thought we'd go to dinner and then a movie . . . sir." Her father replies, "It's 7:00 now. You can eat in thirty minutes. Movies start at 7:30 and last one and a half hours, which means that you can be home by quarter past nine and that gives you fifteen minutes driving time to spare."

At last your date comes downstairs and you rush out the door. Now, ladies, we always want our first date to be perfect. So we choose a restaurant that will impress you so much that you will want to go out with us again. Burger King!

You're trying to shake your nervousness, but it doesn't seem to want to leave. Now the inevitable happens. You dump your drink or drop a ketchup-covered french fry into your lap. It seems that no matter how hard you try, you can't even eat right! And you know that if you can't get a drink or fry to your lips without trouble, there's probably not a chance you'll get near *her* lips.

Finally, dinner is over and you head to the movie. You ask your date, "What movie would you like to see this evening?" Her reply, the standard answer, "Anything would be fine with me!" So you, being the mature gentleman you are, choose a picture and everything seems to be going perfect.

During the movie you are wondering if she really liked the place you chose for dinner or if this is the movie she really wanted to see. No, that's not what you were thinking! You're thinking, I want to hold her hand, I want to put my arm around her, but how do I do it? It's time to apply every reasoning skill you have ever learned. You must utilize all cunning you have developed over the years. It is imperative to be sophisticated and clever. The method you use to hold her hand or put your arm around her must be perfect and fail-proof--one that will entice her to melt in your hands.

Now, there are several ways to accomplish the goal of getting your arm around a sweet young maiden. The first is to be forward and do it. No, we're not man enough.

Another is the standard yawn. Most of us have tried this and know how it's done. The third and final approach is the stretch technique: A large stretch with your arm coming to rest upon her shoulder.

The next challenge, holding her hand. Again we have several options. The first is the direct approach, but, you're still not man enough. Another method to use when trying to hold a girl's hand for the first time is the old, "Look at your lovely fingernails." But by far the most popular approach that most girls have probably experienced is, "My, what a lovely class ring!" Let's face it, guys, we don't care what their class ring looks like, we only want to see if she's got sweaty palms.

Often we never get to date that special someone. The reason, we're afraid of rejection. We're afraid of making that first move in fear of being turned down or being labeled a failure. I promise you that you're better off trying to fulfill a dream than never even taking a chance, because you see, every time we work to achieve a goal, we learn. For every problem, no matter how big or small, there is a solution. Every day of our lives we are faced with challenges. We must learn to deal with these situations in the best way possible and overcome them.

Our next dating challenge was getting the girl to sit next to us in our automobile.

The movie has ended, it's a lovely starlit night, you're driving home and trying to figure how you can get her to sit next to you. Now, if you suffer the same luck that I do, the girls I dated, given a choice, would rather have a wisdom tooth pulled than sit next to me in the car.

I have a solution.

When I was approximately eighteen years old, I discovered the greatest concoction ever invented. I guarantee this product will coax your date into sitting snugly under your arm. There is no way to resist the temptation that this material has over a person. This attractant can be purchased over the counter at your nearest drug store, WalMart, K-Mart or Family Dollar Store without a prescription. Chances are that you have some in your own garage and that your father used it when he was your age. Now this is a closely kept secret, usually passed on from father to son. Women are not to know about it or they will be wary and on the alert. This miracle mixture has used several names in the past, but we all know it simply as... Armor All!

At this moment, most men reading this book are wondering, "How can Armor All help me to be more romantic?" First of all, before your next date or next ride with your spouse, clean your vehicle thoroughly. Take a screwdriver, and from the passenger side, remove the arm rest, the window crank, and the door handle. Now, double check to insure that anything that can be grabbed or held onto is removed. Take your Armor All and, with a clean cloth, spread a smooth coat all across the front seat of your car. (Sorry, this only works with leather or vinyl seats.)

The car I owned when first experimenting with this technique was a 1973 Chevrolet Impala four door. The car was huge! You could load up my two brothers, four sisters, mother, father, grandmother, grandfather, two aunts, one uncle, our family dog and still have room for groceries. My car was definitely a "family cruiser." A sticker on the rear bumper read, "Warning--This vehicle makes wide right turns."

Now is the time for the big test. Pick up your date. If she doesn't sit next to you, it's time for the S.O.B. (Slide Over Baby) turn. The secret, make a sharp right hand turn, and I guarantee your date will slide across the seat and come to rest snugly under your arm!

Every car I owned had the most beautiful seats imaginable due to my extra care to coat them thoroughly with Armour All before every date. However, the door panel on the passenger side was ripped, torn and gouged. The reason? It seems that when I would turn, the sweet, kind, loving, adorable, beautiful, quiet girl sitting next to me would turn into a werewolf. Her fingernails would grow, her arms would become strong, her nostrils would flare and fire would shoot from her eyes when she realized that in a split second she would be sitting under my . . . pit! She would scratch and claw, bite and chew, kick and spin just to keep from sliding across the seat! But in the end the Armour All would prevail and she would sit close to me.

Again, I say, no matter how large or small a problem is, there is a solution. By sharing information we can overcome many of the challenges of life. Most obstacles are overcome through teamwork and communication. When we identify a problem and work diligently to solve it, we can create a more positive environment for our spouses, children, and co-workers. We must take the lead as communicators and act as role models to others. Communication can be verbal as well as nonverbal. We communicate feelings with our actions whether it be our body language, the expressions on our faces, or the way we move.

It was a hot, quiet night, not much different from any other. Suddenly the screeching and crying of a small child shattered the silence. My sister, Kathleen, woke up crying. Her wailing woke the rest of us, and we ran down the hallway to see what was wrong. There stood Kathleen at my father's bedroom door, which was closed. She knocked, and my father responded, "Who's there?" "It's Kathleen," she replied, tears streaming down her cheeks. "Can I come in?" "Come on in," my father answered. In she walked followed by the rest of us, and we were asking one another, "What's wrong with her?"

My father asked, "What's wrong?" Kathleen said, "There's a bug." "Is it in your bedroom?" Dad asked. "No sir," she answered. "Is it in the hallway?" Dad inquired. "No sir," she said. "Is the bug in the bathroom?" Dad persisted. "No sir," Kathleen answered. "Did you dream about this bug?" he asked. "No sir," was her response. My father said, "Kathleen, where is the bug?" She replied, "It's under my arm."

I don't know how a six year old child must sleep to have the pleasure of a bug under her arm, but she did it! As Kathleen stood there in obvious distress, the rest of us broke out in laughter.

Now, my father is a very modest man. Never do I remember my father walking around the house in his underwear. Some people have fathers and husbands who will answer the door or walk out into the front yard and retrieve the morning paper in their "Fruit Of The Looms." Not my father! If we were in his bedroom and he was in bed, he would say, "Hand me my pants." He would slide them under the covers, put them on, and only then emerge from underneath the protection of the sheets.

My father wore boxer shorts. You know, the kind teenage girls wear to the mall. The only time we saw them was when they were in the dryer. It was like television to us. We would look through the window of the dryer and say, "Look at his underwear, they've got polka dots on them."

Imagine, my sister is crying, we're laughing and my father is trying to give her the strength she needs to overcome her fear. He says, "Kathleen, there's no need to be afraid. That bug can't sting you, bite you or hurt you in any way. There's nothing to be afraid of." "But I'm scared, daddy!" she said. "Don't be afraid," he said. Finally, he gave her the strength to overcome her fear. He said, "Honey, lift your arm and let that bug out of its confinement." She lifted her arm and sure enough there was a roach under her arm. However, it didn't land on the floor. It fell onto the bed and went down underneath the covers. I never realized that a middle-aged man could move so quickly. In an instant, he was hovering approximately three feet above the bed, legs spinning in midair, arms flailing wildly about his body, and his voice shrieking, "There's a roach on me, there's a roach on me!" Meanwhile, we're yelling, "Look at his underwear . . . they've got hearts on them!"

I don't know if there is a point to that story. If there is any point whatsoever, it is this: In no way did my father practice what he preached, and he proved it by his actions.

Every one of us is a role model to someone, whether it is a child, spouse, co-worker or someone who admires us from afar. We must take this responsibility seriously and strive to uphold the highest of moral standards and values. We are judged more often based upon our actions than our words. It is more important to lead others based upon what we do than what we say. If you're going to talk it, you'd better walk it and if you walk it, you're going to influence people.

During leadership conferences and camps with business people, educators, and students, we divide delegates into groups of approximately ten members each and have them participate in an activity we call "Breakthrough" (included in the next chapter). During this program, the groups go through a series of questions that allow them, in a very short period of time, to find out a great deal about one another. Every person in every group is required to answer all questions. The questions range from favorite colors, favorite books, and favorite movies to the qualities you look for in a close personal friend, the person who has been the biggest influence upon your life, and what you would wish to do if you had three months left in which to live.

Participating in one particular program was a young lady by the name of Maria. Maria was a great deal like any other student leader attending the program, with the exception of one physical difference--she was missing the middle finger on each hand. Because of this handicap, she was treated as an outsider by most of the participants. Instead of others initiating conversation with Maria, she seemed excluded from the group. Some of those attending centered their conversations around her hands. One young person was overheard saying, "Did you see her hands? That looks awful! I wonder what happened." Another remarked, "I don't know, let's go talk to her." The response, "No way, we might catch it!"

During "Breakthrough" one of the questions posed is, "What do you hate the most?" Of course a wide variety of answers is given. "I hate my little brother, he's such a pain. Everywhere I go, he goes. Then he tells mom and dad everything we do." "I hate homework and studying for tests!" "I hate getting up so early in the morning for school. I think school should start at 11:00, have lunch at 12:00 and be out of there by 1:00."

I said, "Maria, what do you hate the most?" She didn't respond. Maria stared blankly at the floor. "Maria, it's your turn, what do you hate the most?" Tears began streaming down Maria's face. Finally she broke the silence and said, "I hate my father!" She went on to explain why and added, "When I was a little girl, my father got mad at me and he cut my fingers off."

Dead silence! No one could take a breath.

Maria continued, "It was a long time ago, and I really don't remember it happening. Maybe that's good. I was taken from my home and have spent my life so far in foster homes, group homes, and orphanages. Unlike other students, I don't have a place to call home. But the worst part about it is the way that my classmates and strangers treat me. People can be so cruel with the things that they say and the things that they do. Instead of getting to know

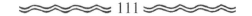

me as a person, they treat me based upon something that is totally beyond my control."

What happened next was truly amazing. Suddenly, a feeling of empathy overcame the group. Now, instead of Maria being an outsider with hands that were different from everyone else's, she became a person. A young lady sitting next to Maria reached out and grasped her hand. The student sitting on the other side of Maria put his arm around her shoulder. One young man on the other side of the circle, stood up, walked over, and gave Maria a hug. They all offered their hands, hearts, love and compassion.

Why? Because now we knew the rest of the story.

What Maria had gone through with her father was a terrible ordeal. As a result, she had to deal with the constant rejection and ridicule of others for the rest of her life. Why? Because she was different in *appearance*. Maria was judged not by what was inside but what showed on the outside.

We have more in common with one another than we might think. Many times we base our opinions of others by the way they look as opposed to the way they think. Everyone on the face of this Earth is different, and that's a wonderful thing. If we all walked the same, talked the same, thought the same, looked the same, and acted the same what a boring place this would be. Instead of concentrating on the negative differences between us, let's look for the positive attributes of others, because I'll promise you, *much greater are the things that unite us than the things that divide us.*

We need to open the lines of communication, get to know our neighbors, and make them friends.

(In the next chapter, I have included a copy of the "Breakthrough" activity.)

BREAKTHROUGH

BREAKTHROUGH

This chapter provides an activity (mentioned in the previous chapter) that can be done individually and/or with two or more people. This exercise fosters self-awareness and an appreciation of others through the use of questions designed to reveal more than superficial conversations include--deeper mutual concerns and insights between family, friends, acquaintances or associates.

Breakthrough gives you a chance to find out more about yourself and others by opening up positively to one another in small groups and provides a vehicle for people to communicate on a "real" level as soon as possible.

It can provide insight into our personal self and assist us to find common bonds between one another that may help to create, strengthen and build close personal relationships.

THIS ACTIVITY IS MOST EFFECTIVE IF THE FOLLOWING PROCEDURES ARE IMPLEMENTED.

1. Have the participants sit in a tight circle with no empty chairs between them.

2. Have each individual introduce him/herself to the group.

3. Each participant must answer every question. They can pass if no answer comes to mind, but must answer before going on to the next question.

4. The group leader should repeat each answer as it is given. This will insure that all participants hear all the answers.

5. Participants cannot repeat answers that another member has given. If someone uses your first answer, when your turn arises, share that answer and then choose a new one.

6. Answer the questions as you hear them and interpret them. React to what you hear.

7. It is not necessary to use all of the sample questions, choose the ones you like and feel free to add questions

not listed in this chapter. (It is suggested to follow the questions in the order in which they are printed.)

8. Do not tell the participants about the "WRAP-UP" beforehand. Switch to the Wrap-up approximately 10 minutes before you wish to stop. Please include these questions as this is where closure happens.

9. The group leader must participate and answer each question as well.

<u>DIRECTIONS</u>
<u>(PLEASE READ OUT LOUD TO THE PARTICIPANTS)</u>

In just a moment we will be answering questions that will help us to learn more about the individuals in our group as well as ourselves. Please answer with the first thought that comes to your mind. There are no wrong answers and every response you give is absolutely correct.

Listen to the questions and answer them the way you understand them. This is not a discussion and no one will question your answers. Following this activity we will have the chance to expand upon responses given and

ask questions of each other on a one on one basis.

Everyone must answer every question. When your turn arises, if you don't have an answer you may "PASS," however, before we go on to the next question we will ask for your response.

I will start with a different person each time and proceed around the circle until everyone responds.

Please speak loud enough for everyone in our group to hear.

Be as honest as you can and don't change your answer to what you think might be more "appropriate."

While each member of our group is answering, observe that individual closely. We can learn a lot from body language, an expression, the fluctuation of their voice and their attitude. We want to find out the good things about one another and provide a foundation upon which we can build relationships.

This is not a discussion. We must listen to one another and try to find out as much as we can about each another as well as ourselves.

We are not required to write anything down, memorize any answers and will not be quizzed on this activity. We are here to be as honest as we can, breakthrough barriers and learn about one another.

QUESTIONS

1. What is your name?

2. Who were you named for or after?

3. Do you have a nickname and if so, how did you get it?

4. Where are you from?

5. When is your birthday?

6. What is your astrological sign?

7. What is your favorite food?

8. What is your favorite drink?

9. What is your favorite dessert?

10. Who is your favorite movie star?

11. What is the best Christmas present you have ever received?

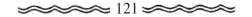

12. What is the best birthday present you ever received?

13. What was your favorite Halloween costume?

14. What is your favorite board game?

15. Did you ever go to a summer camp? If so, what kind?

16. If you could have any type of vehicle, free of charge, what would you choose?

17. Who was or is your favorite school teacher and why?

18. What was or is your high school mascot?

19. Can you speak a foreign language? If so, which one(s)?

20. Do you have a hobby? If so, what is it?

21. What is the name of your favorite restaurant?

22. Are you currently on or have you ever been on any sports teams?

23. Are you or were you in any student organizations in high school or college?

24. What is, or was, your favorite subject in school?

25. Do you play a musical instrument?

26. Would you like to, or have you ever served in the military? If so, which branch?

27. What do you collect?

28. Who is your favorite Disney character?

29. What would be your dream career?

30. Who is your favorite aunt or uncle? Why?

31. What is your favorite candy bar?

32. What flavor of ice cream is your favorite?

33. What kind of cake or pie do you like?

34. How many brothers or sisters do you have and what are their names?

35. Who is your favorite sports team? (college and/or professional)

36. What was your most embarrassing moment?

37. What is your favorite room in your home?

38. Where is the "coolest or neatest" place you have ever been?

39. What one day in your life would you like to live over?

40. What is the best book you have ever read?

41. What is the first movie you remember seeing in a theater?

42. What is the best movie you have ever seen?

43. My favorite musical group is _____.

44. My favorite song is _____.

45. What television show do you like the most?

46. If you could travel any place in the world, where would you go first?

47. If you could choose to be an animal other than man, what animal would you choose to be?

48. If you could build one thing, what would it be?

49. What do you like to do most with a free hour?

50. What is your favorite color?

51. What is the biggest waste you know of?

52. If you could tape record the ugliest thing you know of, what sound would you use?

53. What sound would you use for beauty?

54. Choose a word which best describes your total life up to this moment in time.

55. When do you sense being most alive?

56. What do you think of when you hear the word TRAGEDY?

57. Where were you when: President Kennedy was shot?
Martin Luther King, Jr. was killed?
President Reagan was shot?
The Space Shuttle exploded?
The Federal Building in Oklahoma was bombed?
(Answer all that you can)

58. If you could smash one thing and only one thing, what would you smash?

59. What is the most beautiful thing you have ever seen?

60. Who is your hero?

61. Choose a word to describe a sunset.

62. An outside activity I am active in is _____.

63. My future dreams for myself include _____.

64. What is the most overwhelming thing you know?

65. In your opinion, who was the greatest American in history?

66. What is the greatest problem in the United States?

67. What is the greatest strength of the United States?

68. What future discovery do you anticipate the most?

69. What is the greatest crime one person can commit towards another?

70. What makes you feel most secure?

71. When you think of young children laughing, what comes to mind?

72. What is the most powerful force loose in the world today?

73. What is one thing you would change in your association/business/school/organization?

74. Give another word for God.

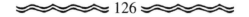

75. What do you hate the most?

76. When do you feel most lonely?

77. What is the kindest thing you have ever seen one person do for another?

78. When you think of children less than three years old, what comes to mind?

79. How many children or grandchildren, if any, would you like to have?

80. Choose a word which you feel describes elderly people.

81. What comes to mind when you hear the word REALITY?

82. Do you have a "pet peeve?" If so, what is it?

83. What is the most honest thing you have known?

84. What is the most beautiful quality about people?

85. If you could paint it, what color is love?

86. On what basis do you select your friends?

87. What do you love the most?

88. What is the greatest value that guides your life?

89. What family member or relative has influenced your life the most?

90. Not including a family member or relative, who has positively influenced your life the most?

91. If you woke up with only one ability and **only** one, what would it be?

92. If you could change places with one person (living or not) for 24 hours, who would that person be?

93. If you could choose to live forever, would you? If yes, why? If no, why not?

94. When you die, what do you want written on your tombstone?

95. If your house caught on fire and all family members and pets are safely out and you had enough time to go in and get only one of your possessions, what would it be and why?

96. If you were told today that you had only three months to live what would you wish or do?

97. How do you want to be remembered?

98. What do you think you have done or wish to do to benefit mankind?

99. What do you feel is your greatest personal accomplishment?

100. Are there any other questions you would like to ask?

WRAP-UP

It is not necessary for every person in the group to answer these questions. Read the following set one at a time and ask for responses from anyone who wishes to answer.

1. Why did we do this?

2. What happened during this session?

3. What things did you find out about other people?

4. What do you hope to accomplish while you attend this conference?

5. Which person did you learn the most about?

6. What person do you want to know better?

7. Which person do you think you could work with best for a long period of time?

8. Which person do you know the least about?

9. Which person likes people the most?

10. Who enjoys life the most?

11. Which answer do you want explained?

12. Which person do you feel is most like you?

GENERALLY
SPEAKING

GENERALLY SPEAKING

EFFECTIVE SPEAKING

*G*enerally speaking, one of the most popular questions asked after presentations is, "How long have you been speaking?" My general response, "Since I was two and a half years old." The fact is, it doesn't matter how long you've been speaking but how effective your presentations are. Are you able to maintain the interest of the audience and convey your message in a manner that is interesting and informative? Are you able to capture your listener's interest and keep their attention throughout your programs?

Most of us have sat in classes, at conferences, and in sessions where the presenter is monotone, boring, dry, dull, tedious, colorless, bleak, lackluster, drab, dismal, dreary, gloomy, glum, dim, flat, lifeless, lethargic, and listless. The most important topic in the world has little value if no one is paying attention. If the speaker's presentation skills lack luster and fail to maintain the interest of the audience, what good is the presentation?

133

We have all left meetings and felt that we wasted our time because, instead of hearing the speaker, our minds wandered to a faraway land and we spent the entire time wishing we were somewhere else. True?

This chapter is an attempt to provide "tips" and suggestions on how we can improve our presentation skills and develop material, transitions and, ultimately, more effective presentations. There are as many ways to develop presentations as there are speakers. It seems that every presenter has his own method of creating material and speeches. The following is the method I have incorporated over the years, and hopefully it will provide thoughts that may be beneficial to you.

DEVELOPING A SPEECH

When it comes time to develop a speech, we must decide what the goals and objectives of the presentation will be. Are we informing the audience? Teaching a lesson? Entertaining? Motivating? Convincing? A combination of all these? Ask yourself some of the following questions:

◆ Who are you addressing?
◆ What is your topic?
◆ What message are you trying to convey?
◆ Who will be in the audience?
◆ What type of speech is this? (informative/instructional/ motivational/inspirational)

To target my audience and to assist in developing presentations, I utilize the questionnaire at the end of this chapter. This is completed by the person or persons booking the presentation via telephone or mail. On several occasions we have even provided a copy of the questionnaire to a few individuals who will be attending the program. This approach provides several viewpoints and additional information to consider when planning programs.

This questionnaire has been an excellent tool to narrow the scope of the presentation and ensure that the goals and objectives of the meeting planner are met and help enormously in planning effective programs.

FORMAT

The typical "format" for speeches that most of us are familiar with is as follows:

- ◆ Introduction - Tell the audience what you're going to tell them.
- ◆ Body - Tell them.
- ◆ Conclusion - Tell them what you told them.

Using this format, however, does depend upon the type of presentation you are delivering. We can implement it when delivering instructional speeches.

♦ Introduction: "Today we are going to learn to gargle peanut butter."
♦ Body: Teach them how to gargle peanut butter.
♦ Conclusion: Review how to gargle peanut butter.

Utilizing the previously mentioned questionnaire as a guide to develop your presentations, create a program that will accomplish the necessary goals and format your speech to meet your goals.

DELIVERY

It is my opinion that there is no exact set of rules we must follow to deliver an effective presentation. Most of the decisions depend on numerous variables that must take into consideration each presenter's individual style and delivery.

DO WHAT WORKS FOR YOU!!!

Every presenter has his own "style." Some speakers are humorous (Jeff Foxworthy, Bill Cosby), some have very dynamic presentation skills (Dr. Martin Luther King, Jr., John F. Kennedy), some have voices that capture their audience's attention (James Earl Jones). What do these presenters do that separates them from the rest? They focus on their talents and abilities and develop their presentations around those skills. They incorporate their own styles into their work.

At the age of twenty-one, Tiger Woods not only won the Augusta National Golf Tournament but set a new course record. After he captured the victory, he was asked if his father, Earl, had given him any words of advice prior to his final round on Sunday. He said, "Yes, my father said, 'Tiger, this will be the most challenging round of golf you have ever played in your life, but if you will be yourself, it will be the most rewarding experience you have ever had!'"

What is *your* style? Are you a humorous person? Can you sing? Will the sound of your voice cause the walls to shake? Do you have other verbal or nonverbal skills that can complement your program? Can you deliver statistics in a fascinating way? Find out what you can do well and develop a presentation that will take advantage of your skills. BE YOURSELF!

Some speakers are comfortable standing behind a podium. Others must walk freely around the stage. Some are more at ease with props or items on stage with them. What do you do best? Do what works for you!

DEVELOPING STORIES

One of the most challenging parts of public speaking is the development of your *own*, unique material. Conventional wisdom says, "If you are trying to make a point, find a story that emphasizes that message." This is true! However, if something has happened in your life

that will benefit others, such a story has value. When something humorous or serious happens to my friend John Marti or myself, we say, "There's a story here somewhere." Look at your life. What are some of the things you remember the most. Perhaps it is something traumatic that happened. Something funny. What was your most embarrassing moment? Did anything happen to a family member or friend that helped you to learn a lesson? Did someone do something for you that really made a difference? If so, what? What experiences have you had over the years that you have learned from?

Though you may not feel that there is any value to the story, write down a few notes that remind you of what actually happened. After you have several story ideas, break out your cassette recorder. Record one story as it actually happened with every detail you can remember. Turn on your computer. Type, word for word, what you have recorded on the cassette tape. Print it and read it. Make additional notations that come to mind as you reread the story and reflect upon the circumstances about which you are writing.

Record the tale again using the additional notes you made on the printed copy. Now update the computer file and reprint it. Review the printed story and delete any unnecessary words. Look for sentences that need to be switched around. Are there any funny punch lines that can be added? Will your audience be laughing or responding to a statement while you are still talking? For example: One story I use occasionally involves the fact that as children, we used to get very excited about getting a new pair of shoes for school. The punch line to this story is, "I remember my father buying me a new pair of shoes for school. I put the old, worn out, dirty, grungy shoes in the box and tied the new shoes tightly to my feet. I knew that I could run faster, jump higher and leap farther than any other kid at school and couldn't wait to show off my new 'kickers.' As we were leaving the store, I asked my father to carry me out so I wouldn't get my new shoes dirty. His reply, 'Son, you're twenty-two years old, it's about time you walked out on your own.'"

Now, the punch line worked, but not as well as I'd hoped. The "zinger" in this joke was, "Son, you're twenty-two years old. . ." The audience would laugh but wouldn't hear me say . . .It's about time you walked out on your own. By writing the story out I found that I could simply switch the line around to, "Son, I think it's time you walked out on your own, you're twenty-two years old."

By hearing and seeing the story we can improve it considerably.

Identify the key words in each sentence. Underline them. Go back and update the computer file. Bold and/or italicize the words that need extra emphasis. Record the story to tape once again as if you were speaking in front of a live audience. Listen to it. Pick it apart. Make corrections and adjustments.

It is amazing how, with this type of effort, you can take a story that you felt had little or no potential and develop it into a featured part of your presentation.

Ask a friend for ideas/stories and get permission to use them. Give credit to the "author." For example, "My friend John Marti shared with me the following experience." They may not know John, but you have given him recognition.

To incorporate humor . . . think funny! Go out of your comfort zone. Observe comedians on television. What do they do to get their audience in a humorous mode? Read funny books. Rent and view humorous movies. Listen to as many speakers as you can (keynote speakers, preachers, teachers, etc.). As we experience these presenters we can begin to develop a "feel" for the skill of incorporating humor and experience its benefits. We can learn a great deal through observing a variety of speakers that will help us to cultivate our own style.

Another helpful technique is to keep a note pad with you and record your thoughts. It is interesting how when we observe a presenter and he or she makes key points, they remind us of something that has occurred in our lives. I'm not suggesting that we "steal" their material but that we create our own with the ideas they help to generate.

How do we know that a new story will be effective the first time we use it? We don't! But the first time you use the illustration in a presentation is not the first time you have shared it. You have told it into your recorder, typed the story into your computer, shared it with friends and family. Practice the story extensively with a constant effort to improve the tale.

Now comes crunch time. The opportunity arrives to deliver the prepared story to a live audience. How can we help to insure that the illustration is effective? If you have two stories that you know work (they can be humorous, serious, dramatic, informative, etc.), place your new story between those two. By doing this, you start off with a great example, proceed to the newly created illustration and come off strong with the second story you know works. If the new story goes well, we complement the others. If the new story "bombs" you are coming off of it strong with the next story.

Record the presentation. Listen to it! Critique the illustration! Improve your examples. Update your computer file. Record it again.

TRANSITIONS

Transitions are the "linking together" of two or more stories in a smooth manner. Effective transition takes preparation and practice. List your stories in an order that seems to make the most sense to you in meeting the criteria of your presentation. Compare each story and decide what they have in common. At this point it is important to make notes on each of the stories that will assist you in "changing gears" and proceeding to your next point. Your transition should be written out, printed, recorded, etc.

A transition can be lengthy or as simple as an extended pause. Regardless, effective transitions can help your presentations flow smoothly and take away the "canned" effect that all speakers must be wary of.

NOTES

Should I use notes? What should my notes consist of? Are notes distracting?

In college I took a public speaking class with a professor who believed that notes for any presentation were unacceptable. However, he kept a notebook full of notes for his presentations to his classes (he called them lesson plans).

Again, I emphasize, DO WHAT WORKS FOR YOU!

Notes should not be so large that they disrupt your presentations (example: Poster sized cue cards.) Nor should they be so small that you must squint, bend over, use a magnifying glass, or learn braille to read them. They *should* be minimal enough to meet your needs and provide a guideline for your presentation. If you prepare your programs by recording and printing them, one or two

words can keep you on track and help you to feel more at ease.

Have you ever been speaking with a friend and your mind went blank? You said something like, "I had something to say but forgot what it was." This can happen during presentations and the satisfaction of knowing that you do have a "crutch" to lean on can make a significant difference. Notes can also assist you in changing your program around in order to maintain the interest of the audience. There may come a point where you must "change gears" and do something differently to invoke interest. You can quickly scan your stories and choose another direction in which to go. Notes will also assist you in making sure that key points are not skipped or forgotten.

Notes for presentations are not for everyone, but by using our own styles, preparing, and practicing, we can determine what works for each of us.

SHOW TIME!

Following are some tips on how to improve live presentations, arrange a meeting room and test a sound system.

First, arrive at least one hour ahead of time. Meet the meeting planner, president, or person in charge. This will give you an opportunity to "case" the room setup and

check the sound system. Take some time to get your final thoughts in line and focus on the upcoming presentation.

HAVE A FRIEND ATTEND THE PROGRAM - This individual can keep notes on things such as response of the audience, volume of your voice, inflection, the number of times you say "um," etc. Ask him or her to record what you did correctly as well as offer constructive suggestions.

AUDIO TAPING - Bring a cassette recorder to presentations with you and record your program. If your speech includes audience response (laughter, sing-a-long, answers to questions, etc.), record the audience. This can be done by placing your recorder microphone in front of the loud speaker, facing the people. The microphone will pick up your voice coming out of the speaker and, by facing it towards the audience, pick up their response. Listen to the tape as you drive home and critique your program based upon the response of the audience, content of the speech, voice tone and inflection, things you did right and areas that you can improve upon.

VIDEO TAPING - Place a video camera in the middle or rear of the room facing the speaker platform. Before your program begins, hit the record button and videotape the full-length presentation. Take advantage of the first opportunity to review the tape. My suggestion for both the audiotape and video tape is to listen to them and/or watch them when you are alone. Most people are very self-conscious about the way they sound or look on tape. When we watch with a friend or family member, we tend to be overcritical of the presentation. Review the tape alone and write brief statements about what you did well and, again, areas that can be improved. In addition, give the tape to someone you respect and ask him or her to review it objectively and to give you a list of suggestions. Video taping is the most effective tool you can use since you will hear your voice, see your body movements and give a clear idea of what your audience hears and sees.

___SOUND SYSTEMS___ - It continues to amaze me the number of times speakers attempt to present to a large group on a podium sound system built for a small room filled with six people. *The greatest speakers in the world are no good if the audience cannot hear them.* Check out the sound system ahead of time. Make sure that there is no feedback, limited echo and that the cord for the microphone is free if you intend to walk around. Practice speaking at the level you are going to use when addressing the group. Remember, the number of people present will determine the sound level. Speaking in an empty room is much different than in one filled with "bodies." You may want to increase the volume of the system slightly to compensate for sound that is absorbed by those present.

Make sure that if you "travel" while you talk that you look at the ceiling above you. Most hotels and conference centers utilize speakers that are placed in the ceiling throughout the room. If you walk under one of those

WHO PACKS THE PARACHUTE?

speakers it may "feed sound" directly into your microphone, therefore causing severe feedback that will send your audience squealing into another area of the conference center for relief.

Walk to the rear of the room and have someone else speak into the microphone (you are now hearing what your audience hears). If you have an opportunity to stand at the back of the room during opening remarks by the president or other key individuals, listen to the echo and sound level. Be sure to watch the audience and determine if there are any "blind" spots (i.e. areas that the audience cannot see or hear you well if you stand there). Examples of blind spots are pillars, room dividers, large plants, etc. If there is an echo, you may want to speak more slowly, therefore minimizing the echo.

Make sure that the people attending the program can hear you loudly and clearly. If they can't, your chances for success are severely diminished.

ROOM SETUP

By arriving on location early, you have some control, in many instances, over the setup of the meeting room. You want your audience up close and personal. Put limited distance between the stage and the front row of the audience. The greater the distance between the speaker and the audience, the greater obstacle you must overcome.

Generally speaking, the more people you have in a smaller room, the more effective the presentation. For example, have you ever been to see a humorous movie in an empty theater? Compare that to seeing a humorous movie in a packed theater. Most often, laughter breeds laughter, and the packed house is more fun. It is better to speak to 200 people in a room built for 175 people than to speak to 200 people in a perfectly-designed auditorium built for 2,000.

Most individuals, given a choice, will sit at the back of the auditorium or meeting room leaving the front ten rows empty. A couple of things to do to help eliminate this problem is to, first, find out how many people are registered or expected. If you have 100 people attending the program and 150 seats set up, remove 50 seats ahead of time.

Bring a roll of masking tape to the presentation with you. Before the people enter the auditorium, count off 50 seats at the rear of the auditorium and tape off those rows. This is much easier than asking everyone to move forward. You and I both know that once we are seated comfortably, we do not want to move.

With the advances in technology, more and more meeting planners are providing their presenters with cordless, microphones. If you are comfortable using this type of equipment, use it. On many occasions when I have given programs, the audience has been sitting in the back of the room with a rather large number of empty rows at the front of the room prior to my program. In those instances I may walk to the back of the room and ask the audience to turn their chairs around. Now those in the rear are in the front. This generates a lot of laughter as well.

Implement your own ideas and be willing to step outside of your comfort zone to try things that are new.

ROOM TEMPERATURE

Room temperature is extremely important. David Letterman keeps his theater on the brink of freezing, because a cool audience is a responsive audience.

Hot, stuffy meeting rooms typically put people to sleep and make them lethargic. Arrive ahead of time and adjust the temperature of the room. Keep in mind that if you have a large audience, the body heat they generate will drive the air temperature up. Don't freeze them, but keep them cool, then light them on fire with your dynamite presentation!

DO IT!

Utilizing these ideas will help to provide a foundation upon which you can build your programs. Be willing to take risks, try things that are new, go outside of your comfort zone, and incorporate your personality and unique style into your programs, and you can't miss.

Break a leg!
Break a leg!!
Break a leg!!!

Page 1 of Questionnaire

"TNT"
Questionnaire

Please complete and return this questionnaire to:
P.O. Box 471771
Charlotte, NC 28247-1771
Phone: (800) 862-1660

Organization/Company name: _____
Contact person: _____
Phone: (__) _____Office
              (__) _____Emergency
              (__) _____Fax
              _____E-mail
Date(s) & day(s) of presentation: _____
Time of session/meeting at which Patrick will be speaking?
_____

Approximately what time will Patrick's presentation begin?
_____
_____

Length of presentation(s): _____
_____

Location of presentation (hotel/convention center): _____
_____
_____

_____Phone #: (__) _____
Suggested speaker attire: *casual*   *suit*   *formal*
% _____Male   % _____Female
Approximate ages: _____
How will the meeting room be arranged?
        _____ Theater style
        _____ Classroom style (chairs with rows of tables)
        _____ Banquet style (round tables)
        _____ Other

Page 2 of Questionnaire

General description of attendees: _____
_____
_____
_____

Will guests be present? Yes/No
If yes, approximately how many? _____
What is the theme of your meeting? _____
_____
_____
_____

What type of meeting is this? _____
_____
_____
_____

What do you perceive as the greatest "need" for your audience? _____
_____
_____
_____

What would you describe as the greatest "fear" for this audience?
_____
_____
_____

Please list any "victories" for this group: _____
_____
_____
_____

What would you like covered in this presentation? _____
_____
_____
_____
_____
_____

Page 3 of Questionnaire

What are your goals/objectives for the next year? _____
_____
_____
_____

What are some of the challenges that your delegates are facing?
_____
_____
_____

What are some of the specific goals (mission statement) of your
organization? _____
_____
_____
_____

Will there be anyone in attendance (known to most of those present)
that you would like to have Patrick incorporate into his presentation
in a humorous way?

    Executive Director/CEO/President: _____
    Single male: _____
    "Class clown": _____
    Married couple: _____
    Other: _____
    Other: _____

Other information: _____
_____
_____
_____

**Please provide any additional information on your organization
that may be helpful to Patrick in personalizing his presentation.**

Thank You!!!
If you have any questions, please give us a call!!!

THE
CUSTODIAN

THE CUSTODIAN

O n April 14, 1997, I had the privilege of addressing a group of parents, educators, business people, and students in Brevard, North Carolina. The purpose of the program was to celebrate a very successful year. Transylvannia County Schools provided a banquet for these individuals and used the evening as a tool to recognize graduating seniors for their outstanding accomplishments during the past year. The high school auditorium was packed, standing room only. Even the aisles had people standing.

Prior to and during my presentation, I noticed that, spaced neatly along the edge of the stage, were approximately a hundred red marble apples. My thought was that they were strictly for decoration and made that comment to Dr. Richard Jones, the Superintendent of Schools. His response was that they were for more than decoration, and I would find out momentarily.

After recognizing the senior class with scholarship presentations and awards for outstanding achievements, a man named Paul Averette approached the stage and announced that it was time for the highlight of the evening. He continued by pointing out the marble apples lining the stage and shared with the audience the following information. "Ladies and gentlemen, the time has come to recognize outstanding individuals in the business of education. We have asked all the graduating seniors to submit the name of one person and only one who during their time in school, has been an outstanding influence upon his or her life. Again, we emphasize that each student nominated one person, not two, not five, only one! We have taken the names of these outstanding people, tallied the results, and in just a moment will recognize those individuals."

He continued by adding, "When we call the name of a person, we ask him or her to please come and stand at the front of the auditorium. We will then ask the graduating seniors who submitted your name to please come forward and present you with your apple."

Mr. Averette proceeded by calling the name of an outstanding educator, and that teacher came to the front. The graduates then came forward and presented the instructor with an apple, a special gift of appreciation, handshakes, and hugs.

The announcer called, "Mr. John Keenan," and the audience fell quiet. Slowly a lady and two children came

forward, smiles on their faces, but tears streaming down their cheeks.

The announcer continued, "Mr. Keenan was a coach here at Brevard High School. We are saddened that Mr. Keenan passed away two years ago and is greatly missed. Would those submitting the name of Mr. John Keenan please come forward."

Four young people rose from the audience, came to the front, and presented Mrs. Keenan, her daughter Sherry, and son Michael with their token of appreciation. The audience erupted in applause.

What an amazing experience it was to see so many people showing such gratitude to outstanding citizens and educators of their community and what rewards and memories those recognized will have for an entire lifetime. Kindergarten teachers, middle school staff and administrators, coaches, club advisors, and band directors were honored.

Toward the end of the evening, Mr. Averette called the name of Mr. Robert Owen. Again, the audience fell silent. Down the center aisle of the high school auditorium came Mr. Owen. He was a gentleman who had a gleam in his eyes, a smile on his face, and a look of amazement that his name had been called.

Dr. Jones, the Superintendent, said, "That's amazing! Do you know who that man is?" My reply, "No Sir, who is he?" Dr. Jones said, "You'll find out in a moment."

When Mr. Owen reached the front and turned to the audience, a look of appreciation and admiration could be seen on every face.

The announcer continued, "Would all the graduating seniors who submitted the name of Mr. Robert Owen as having a tremendous positive impact upon their lives, please come to the front."

Five students, more than any other that evening, approached Mr. Owen and greeted him with hugs, handshakes, pats on the back, and tokens of appreciation. The audience once again exploded in applause, many coming to their feet. The thrill was contagious and the room electrified.

"For those of you who do not know Mr. Owen," the announcer continued, "he works at the high school. He's our custodian!"

The custodian from the high school.

What should this tell us? We should realize that everyone's job is important. Whether you are the chief executive officer of a major corporation, a secretary, a sales representative, an officer of an organization, a member of an association, or, yes, a custodian. Whatever we do in this life, we have an opportunity on a daily basis to influence others in a very positive manner. In many instances, the impact we have upon others is not always immediate nor can it be measured on a scale. But let us not forget the individuals, like Mr. Keenan and Mr. Owen, who do a tremendous job and go far and above the call of duty to be of service to others. We should make a vow to ourselves, like Transylvannia County Schools, that we will tell those in our lives who make a difference what great people they are.

History continues to show that great leaders have first been great servers.

We all have the capability to contribute to the well-being of others and to use our own unique talents and skills to create futures.

At the age of two and a half, my brother Bill was finally "potty trained." Now, like most mothers, ours liked to point out the accomplishments of her children and give them recognition for a job well done. When people would visit our home, mom would say, "Billy, tell them what you can do." He would bow out his chest with pride and say, "I can go to the bathroom all by myself." People would smile and congratulate him on his new "skill."

Eventually the new wore off of the old trick, and the references to his bathroom habits slowly diminished. One

day my mother was in Sears shopping, accompanied by Bill. After a time of shopping, Bill disappeared. My mother had been in the store numerous times and didn't worry too much; however, as she began seeking him out, she could not find him. She checked in the toy department, he wasn't there. She checked by the elevators and escalators, still no Bill. Mom even looked under the dresses of mannequins (little boys get into some strange places). Yet, once again, no Bill.

Just before she panicked, my mother noticed a large group of people gathered in the corner of the store. She decided to walk over and see what was so exciting. Women were giggling, children were snickering, and store employees were calling to one another, "Come over here!" All were engrossed in the activities taking place in this particular area. My mother gently pushed her way through the crowd, and there to her shock and dismay was my brother Bill. He was *sitting* on a display toilet. My mother then did the same thing that most mothers and most of us would do--she turned and quickly walked the other way.

She failed to recognize my brother for doing exactly what he was instructed, trained, and encouraged to do. She couldn't hide for long because Bill ran right up to her and said, "Mommy, guess what I did all by myself!" People were clapping and cheering him on, saying, "Go son, go!"

As managers of people, officers in organizations, educators and/or parents, do we sometimes fail to recognize the accomplishments of others? Many times words of encouragement from others can make the difference in the performance of individuals. We can choose to point out the positive accomplishments of others, or we can choose to point out the negative. We can choose to recognize what's right, or we can bring attention to what's wrong.

I'm not suggesting that we should not give constructive criticism to others when the need arises, but we should try to balance the scale by giving affirmative responses as well. I firmly believe that if we will assume the attitude of directing attention to people that accomplish feats every day, we can increase output and optimism in the workplace and our homes and create a more productive environment. **If you show me a happy workplace, I'll show you a productive workplace**. An environment where people enjoy working with their supervisors and peers will encourage them to work harder for the continued success of their businesses and organizations.

During an interview, Sam Walton, founder of WalMart, was asked, "Mr. Walton, what do you feel is one key to the tremendous success of your company?" Mr. Walton replied, "The associates who work so hard as a team. I also sneak through the stores and try to catch someone doing something **RIGHT**. And when I, or one of our managers, catch someone doing something right, we recognize that person and the smiles come to their faces and that small bit of recognition spreads from associate to associate all the way down to the customer. It's a win-win situation."

When we discuss the importance of providing assistance and being of service to others, we must emphasize the necessity of providing outstanding service as we are representing ourselves, our organizations and our businesses. We must consistently attempt to go above and beyond the call of duty to meet the needs of our clients in order to insure a continued relationship with those for whom we work.

Our attitudes, good or bad, in the workplace have a tremendous impact upon the environment in which we work and can affect our co-workers as well as our customers.

Are we providing top-notch service or barely fulfilling our responsibilities and doing just enough to get by?

Most of us can recall the first time we left home for summer camp, a church program, a conference or college. It was a time when we could expand our horizons, develop skills and/or become more independent, and it provided our mothers the opportunity to "clean" our bedrooms.

After I left home to attend the University of Florida, my mother called one afternoon to see how college life was treating me and to update everything that had been happening at home. She said, "While cleaning up your bedroom, I found something in your dresser drawer." I gulped, my voice squeaked, and I asked, "What did you find?" She paused and said, "I found a shoe repair ticket from Jackson's Shoe Repair." Relieved and able to breathe again, I said simply, "Oh!" Mom informed me that the ticket was over a year old and asked, "Do you remember picking your shoes up?" "Mom, I don't even remember dropping any shoes off to be fixed," I said. She told me that she would be in town tomorrow and would stop by to check on this ticket.

The next evening my mother called and informed me that she'd stopped by the shoe repair shop. "Did they have my shoes?" I asked. "Well," she responded, "I gave Mr. Jackson the ticket, he looked at it and said, 'Mrs. Grady, this ticket is over a year old. We typically only keep unclaimed items 30 days before we discard them.' I know, but would you check just in case they're still here?" Mr. Jackson told her he would. My mother said that he walked into the back room of the shop. She could hear him moving things around, knocking items off the shelf so that dust was literally coming out into the lobby. He returned a few minutes later. "Mom," I asked, "Did he have my shoes?" She said, "Yes, they'll be ready Thursday!"

How often, I wonder, do we do the same thing with jobs we know must be done. Do we procrastinate to the point that we put unnecessary pressure upon ourselves and those depending upon us? Do we delay completing projects in a timely manner or do we set deadlines and strive to meet them or beat them?

I have attempted, over the last several years, to adopt a **DO IT NOW** attitude. When the time comes to work on a task, instead of putting it off until tomorrow, I say to myself, "DO IT NOW!" By doing this, it seems that the burden of meeting deadlines is not as stressful and jobs are being completed more efficiently and ahead of schedule.

In January, 1996, we were in the process of completing our first of two annual mailings to potential clients. Now, in order to market the services of speakers, we send approximately 7,000 brochures, letters and excerpt tapes to clients nationwide. These mailings provide a catalyst by which organizations become familiar with presentations and a method by which to contact our office.

In order to provide the best customer service that we can, when I'm at home in Charlotte, North Carolina, but not in the office, we forward my business line to my cell phone. This way, clients can reach me when I am running errands, in meetings, and so on.

On this particular day, I went to the Post Office, our *"TNT"* company checkbook in hand, cell phone in my jacket pocket with calls forwarded, to purchase stamps for the mailings. We send all correspondence first class, since we deal with first class people. Upon arriving at the

Carmel Commons Post Office, there were about 20 people in line and only two clerks working. Now, if there are two things most people dislike, one is renewing drivers licenses and the other is standing in excessively long lines at the post office, grocery store, or other places of business.

Time is important, so I decided to jump in the car and travel to the Pineville Post Office. This particular location was much smaller, so the service would be more personal, right?

Upon arriving at the Post Office and entering, I found eight people in line and only **one** clerk working. As I mentioned, time is important and I couldn't afford to waste any more, so I decided to stand in line and take my chance.

Finally, after about ten minutes, it was my turn. The clerk at the counter said, "One moment please," opened the cash drawer and began counting the money to insure that the drawer balanced before going on break. Another clerk stood behind the original clerk but did not open another register. Needless to say, people in line were irritated with the additional delay.

Eventually, after the money in the drawer was counted, balanced, and removed, the new clerk placed a tray in the drawer, looked at me, and snapped, "What do you need?" I stepped forward and said, "I need 7,000 first class stamps!" The clerk, with an awful expression on his face, replied disgustedly, "We don't have that many!" (I was

thinking that maybe I should have gone to the drug store with a car full of change and used the dispenser machine.) I replied, "Will you please check?" The clerk, smacked his lips and quipped, "Just a minute!" and disappeared into the back. Meanwhile, people in line were aggravated by yet another delay and began to grumble. I, on the other hand, was embarrassed to be the cause of the holdup.

After a few minutes, the clerk returned with something I had never seen. The clerk had two large rolls of 3,000 stamps and 10 rolls of 100 stamps. The clerk then announced, "We don't have enough!" I replied, "You have more than enough, if you will give me those two rolls of 3,000, that would be 6,000, and ten rolls of 100 stamps would be a 1,000 for a total of 7,000 stamps." "That's not right," said the clerk. "Yes it is," I replied, "3,000 plus 3,000 is 6,000 and ten rolls of 100 is a 1,000 for a grand total of 7,000." "No, that's not right," said the clerk, "Wait here, I'll be back."

Again, another delay and the customers behind me began to huff and puff.

Finally, the clerk appeared again and announced, "Here's what we're going to do, we're going to give you these ten rolls of 100 stamps, that's 1,000, another roll of 3,000 stamps for a total of 4,000 and finally another roll of 3,000 for a total of 7,000." "Fine!" I replied.

The clerk then started punching the buttons on the cash register and announced that my total would be $2,240.00. I filled out and handed the clerk our company check along with my drivers license. The clerk then announced, "We can't take this check." "Why can't you take the check," I asked. His response, "It's a business check." I told the clerk that I wrote business checks for stamps all the time, that's the way we pay bills this large. "Do you have any other identification?" he asked. I pulled out credit cards, AAA card, insurance card, social security card, airline frequent flier cards, rental car cards, calling cards, and a picture of my wife and child.

"Do you have any other identification?" asked the clerk. I said, "I can get my mother on the phone if you'd like." "Wait here," said the clerk, and stepped to the cubicle next to the one at which I stood.

Now, the people in line were very angry! I was terribly embarrassed and aggravated, and I believe the postal clerk was totally confused.

Of all the times in the world for my cell phone to ring, this was not a very good time for a client to catch me, for I was not in the best of moods. But, as I mentioned previously, customer service is extremely important, positive attitude a necessity, for you never know who is on the other end of the line.

I reached into my jacket pocket, pulled out the phone, and in the most enthusiastic voice I could muster at the time and said, "Hello, Patrick Grady." Pause. The voice on the other end was very familiar and said, "Is this *TNT*?" Pause. "Yes it is," I said.

I had heard this voice before, but who was it? That's it! That's it! I knew that voice! On the other end of the line was the clerk from the post office!

"Do you have somebody named Patrick Grady working for you?" asked the clerk. "Yes, we do," I replied. "Did you send him to the post office to buy stamps," he asked. "Yes, we did, 7,000 of them," I said. "Is he supposed to have the company checkbook," asked the clerk. "Yes, he is," I answered. "Very well," replied the clerk. "Oh, one other thing," I added, "Patrick has a very, very short temper. Whatever you do, don't make him mad! He might go . . . *postal*!" There was a rather lengthy pause and then a gulp on the other end of the line. The clerk said, "Thank you" and hung up the phone. He then walked over to me, pushed the stamps in my direction, smiled and in a very pleasant voice said, "Have a nice day." I grabbed the stamps and ran out of the post office.

The people waiting in line had heard **both** ends of the conversation and were laughing out loud.

Attitude! The customer service attitude was wrong from the moment I walked into the post office. That failure, on behalf of the clerk, to show appreciation for the customer, affected everyone in line. From the start, the demeanor of the clerk had an immediate effect upon all customers and affected everyone's outlook about the entire United States Postal Service.

Now, I realize that everyone can have a bad day; however, there is no excuse for the negative conduct of one individual to ruin the good reputation that companies and organizations work for years to develop. Too many individuals labor intensively to create a positive reputation to have one individual destroy it. One person with a pessimistic outlook can demolish what took years to create. Let us remember when working for an organization that "bad news travels like wildfire."

If we don't provide top quality, enthusiastic customer service, someone else will.

WHO PACKS THE PARACHUTE?

WHO PACKS
THE PARACHUTE?

C hange--a six-letter word that puts fear in the hearts
of millions of individuals throughout the entire
world. Why? Because too often we worry about
the negative aspects of some change instead of the positive
ways in which it can be of benefit to all of us. As leaders
and managers, however, we must be open to the ideas of
others, to listen to the thoughts of those we are leading,
and to weigh the benefits that change can offer.

By listening to the opinions of others we can accumulate
knowledge and implement educated decisions. We can
also, by seeking out creative thoughts from our peers,
come up with suggestions that may help our organizations
and businesses to reach higher goals.

Times, though, are changing constantly, and we must make
modifications on a continuous basis. When NASA first
flew astronauts to the moon, they were off course 90% of
the time, and they had to constantly adjust their flight
plan to meet their objective successfully. It is the same in

both our personal and professional lives. The ability to adapt to change provides for survival of the fittest.

My first job, after graduating from college, was that of educator. I taught vocational agriculture and had the responsibility of teaching students about animal production, crop production, horticulture, welding, and numerous other skills associated with the industry of agribusiness.

Our school had a twenty-five-acre school farm upon which we could implement many of the ideas taught in the classroom. This was a way to join book knowledge with "hands on" application. On the school farm we had cattle, my horse, several sheep, pigs, and a few chickens. The purpose was to give students the opportunity and responsibility of learning to care for livestock and also to discover where our food comes from. It was the first time many of them realized that individuals had to produce the products we consume, that such products don't just "magically" show up at the grocery store or in restaurants.

One afternoon a water line in a hog pen was broken by one of the pigs. Water was pouring from the pipe, and it needed mending. Never one to pass up the opportunity to "teach" others, I brought the entire class down to the pen, gathered them around, and announced, "We're going to make a learning experience out of this!"

Turning to one student I said, "Curtis, please go behind the barn and shut off the water at the main valve." Curtis was gone for several minutes, and the water continued to bubble rapidly from the ground. Eventually, he shouted, "Mr. Grady, which direction do I turn it?" The entire class chuckled and I responded, "Curtis, turn it clockwise." There was a brief delay and then a response when he said, "Mr. Grady, I've got a digital watch." Of course, our laughter could be heard all the way back to the school. One of the students called back to him, "Curtis, righty tighty, lefty loosey!"

This experience emphasizes that times are changing and technology is making tremendous advances in creating ways that we can do our jobs better, easier, and more efficiently. One method to keep up with change is to incorporate the talents, skills, and knowledge of our associates. By doing this we can tap into the creative energy that each individual in our corporations and organizations possesses.

When my neighbor's daughter Holly was six years old, she and her friend Meghan stopped by for a brief visit one summer afternoon. Our doorbell rang and at the door stood the two young ladies. Holly had in her hand a small sign that read, "LOST KITTEN - IF FOUND CALL 542-5116." With great concern I asked, "Holly, did you lose your kitty?" She replied, "No sir, but if you find one, we want it!" How ingenious! I laughed and thought how cute they looked with the sign in their hand and the anticipation of finding a kitty on their faces.

I imagined that they were sitting around brainstorming that morning and said, "I'd like a kitten, but how can we get one?" They probably then started sharing ideas and eventually settled on this plan. Sharing this story with Holly's father Jay, who is also our veterinarian, we both agreed that this was a classic, memorable experience and quite clever as well. But would it work?

Within a week, Holly received a call and got her kitten!

Creativity! We must listen to the ideas of others. Perhaps in some of our bizarre thoughts there is information that we can use to accomplish our goals and objectives. We need to use our imaginations, share our thoughts, and listen to as many people as possible when trying to solve problems. The suggestions of others, whether they are corporate executives, managers, associates, or dock workers, can save our companies money as well as precious time. In many instances we can incorporate their thoughts into our plans to better accomplish our goals.

More and more corporations worldwide are investing in creativity workshops, seminars that get the "creative juices" flowing and the imagination off and running. During these sessions, associates, managers, and C.E.O.s work together as equals in a casual atmosphere, but most importantly they *listen* to one another no matter how off the wall their thoughts might be. Groups can be seen throwing toys back and forth, squirting one another with Silly String and water guns, eating cotton candy, and sitting and lying on the floor. From these sessions come ideas for new products and thoughts on the direction the companies would like to take.

One toy developer and manufacturer takes this activity a step further. They bring in elementary students from their local schools and play games. The corporate managers and product developers sit on the floor, wear clown noses, kick off their shoes, chase one another around the room, and have a great time. They also distribute a number of toys to the group and ask the young people to play with them. As the afternoon progresses, they start asking children questions:

- ◆ "What do you think of this toy?"
- ◆ "What would make this item better and more fun to play with?"
- ◆ "What do you like about this toy?"
- ◆ "What don't you like about this toy?"
- ◆ "What toys would you like to have?"
- ◆ "What are some of the qualities you look for in toys you purchase?"

This activity is very similar to events in the movie, *"Big"* starring Tom Hanks. By getting feedback and input from actual consumers, the company is able to create new products, incorporate the ideas of the children to make

existing products better, work on developing future products, and meet the needs of their customers. Granted, some of the ideas presented are farfetched and perhaps not possible. But certain ideas are discussed, fine-tuned, expanded upon, and utilized.

Several years ago the paper manufacturing company Georgia Pacific implemented a program that not only encouraged employee input, but rewarded that feedback as well. Management asked associates working in their plants and on assembly lines to fill out evaluation/ suggestion forms on ways to make their jobs easier. The objective was to find ways that jobs could be completed more efficiently and create a more productive and positive work environment. The ideas were reviewed with employees by department heads and passed on to committees that evaluated the recommendations. An associate who contributed an idea was included in decision-making and assisted in explaining the suggestion. Those suggestions the company felt had merit were given further review by management, and a determination was made as to whether to implement the change or not. If the final decision was to implement the suggestion, the associate who contributed the idea received a financial reward for his or her effort.

This program allowed Georgia Pacific to make employees an integral part of the decision-making process and boosted their involvement on both a production level and management level. This had several effects. Associates felt better about themselves and developed a sense of pride for their contribution, and the corporation was able to save money by implementing many of the ideas their people contributed.

Whether we are in sales, production, management, or education or provide a service to others, we can implement ideas such as this. As we strive to discover goals for any and all organizations we work with, we can more successfully attain these goals by getting input from others.

When we set goals for our organizations, we must also determine how to achieve them and if in fact they are realistic.

There is an old story about a first grade teacher who passed out to her students a picture of a duck carrying an umbrella. She also gave the students crayons and asked them to do their best coloring the picture. Then, like most good teachers, she proceeded around the room to compliment their work and offer constructive criticism. She looked at one young man's picture and said, "Oh, Matthew, that's a pretty yellow duck!" She peered over Erin's shoulder and said, "Erin, you're doing a great job staying in the lines, and you've chosen such pretty colors!" Next, she walked up to Caleb and quipped, "Now, Caleb! Caleb, when was the last time you saw a purple duck with red and green polka dots?" Caleb looked up and responded,

"When is the last time you saw a duck carrying an umbrella?"

This anecdote illustrates the importance of realistic goals. Again, I emphasize the importance of setting goals that are researched and possible to attain. They should not necessarily be simple goals, but they must be goals that can be accomplished by working together as a team.

As a young child, I, like many of my friends, had the dream of one day playing professional baseball, a dream so real I could almost hear the crack of the bat, the roar of the crowd, the smell of the popcorn and taste the hot dogs.

As the time for little league tryouts quickly approached, my friend Jim and I practiced almost daily. Jim was the pitcher and I the catcher. Finally the big day arrived. We showed up at the field early, dressed in our cleats and carrying our freshly-oiled gloves. We started warming up. Jim would pitch one; I'd catch it and throw it back. The announcement was made that we had five minutes before the actual tryouts would begin. The butterflies were now flying, and the excitement of beginning my journey to the major league was under way.

Jim made an announcement, "Watch out for my curve ball." My reply, "Fifth graders can't throw curve balls." He wound up, reared back and let it fly! The cry of the umpire was drifting through my mind, "Strike three!" I was lost in a world of screaming fans, dusty diamonds, and it all seemed so real! When I finally regained consciousness, and the trees, sky, and gawking fifth graders stopped spinning around, I realized painfully that I had caught the ball with my right eye.

One of the volunteers sent for a bag of ice, and I spent the rest of the tryouts sitting on the bench with this cold concoction stuck to my brow.

At the end of the day the picks were announced. Yes, I had been chosen--LAST! My team – Hooper Funeral Homes. I didn't want to play for Hooper Funeral Homes. Oh, the jokes we'd have to put up with. "Here comes Hooper Funeral Homes, their team is dead!" "We're going to kill you, but look on the bright side--at least you'll have someone to bury you!" "We're going to plant you six feet under." "Hooper Funeral Homes, your team is a bunch of stiffs!"

This is not how dreams are supposed to start out. Everything was supposed to go perfectly. We did play that year. We won a few games and came in second in many more. Overall, we had a wonderful time, and it was a great learning experience.

The next year, I decided, would be different.

We were now sixth graders. We had matured, grown, and were now ready to avenge ourselves and be chosen to lead our teams to the championship. The day arrived.

We would now begin our second year in little league. Why we were almost veterans. We knew how the system worked. Some of us were even developing the ability, while in the outfield, to watch the ball instead of chasing butterflies.

Once again, Jim and I were warming up; Jim pitching and me catching. Five more minutes until start time. We *knew* we were number one draft picks. No coach in his right mind would pass up the opportunity to have us on his team. Why, if they didn't select us in the first round, we were sure that they'd be run out of town dragging their belongings behind them.

Here came Jim's announcement. "Watch out for my curve ball." Again, my reply, "Sixth graders can't throw curve balls." It wouldn't happen again. There was no way I'd stop the ball using my right eye. I was ready. He wound up, reared back, spun around, and flung the ball right to me. This time, I was ready! I kept my eye on the ball the entire time until it struck. Not my right eye, but the left.

Again, a search for ice and a clean place on the bench upon which I would lie until the end of the day. My dream of playing major league baseball was quickly becoming a fantasy. And yes, once again, I was the last pick to play for Hooper Funeral Homes.

I decided right then and there, next year, I'd warm up with a better pitcher.

We finished that season, and I played again in the seventh grade but soon lost interest in pursuing the major leagues. And indeed, all was not lost because I realized it was better to have pursued the dream than never to have even tried. I also came to understand that the ability to play baseball was not natural to me. More importantly, I realized that the desire, dedication, and willingness to work hard to develop the little skill I did have was not a priority. I was not completely sold on the idea that I could in fact make baseball a career, nor was I willing to work and work hard to make this particular dream a reality. My next step was to search for something about which I could be passionate. Through the help and encouragement of my parents, teachers, and friends, I pursued other interests. Eventually, I became involved in a number of organizations in our community and school and found my niche. I participated in public speaking contests that would eventually lead to a full-time speaking career.

As we set personal, family and professional goals in life we must occasionally step back, reevaluate, rethink, replan, and retry. We must learn to set short-term projects that will serve as stepping stones toward eventual major objectives. The short-term goals become stepping stones to success and a way by which we can judge our accomplishments and see immediate results.

We live in a time of continuous change in the workplace. Technological advances can assist us to do our jobs more easily and efficiently, so it is necessary to try and keep up with these changes and find ways to incorporate them into our daily routines. Investing in our people and providing an opportunity for them to receive training and become more knowledgeable can create better working conditions and reduce the stress associated with change. We must continue to empower individuals to do a job and delegate responsibilities to associates. As managers we are wise to keep progress reports on projects others are directing so that we continually know where we stand and in which direction we wish to proceed.

By recognizing the strengths and weaknesses of our employees, we can place them in positions where they can excel at the jobs they do. It is also important to create teams that are compatible and work together in a unified fashion and give them the opportunity to express their comments and concerns. We must provide comfortable work environments where people are held responsible for tasks and recognized for accomplishments.

One way to help create a more enthusiastic work environment is to put some humor back into the workplace. Several years ago I was on a USAirways flight from Dallas, Texas, to Charlotte, North Carolina. The flight was the last of the day, a late evening flight that arrived in North Carolina close to midnight. It was apparent that those boarding the aircraft were tired from a long day's work and traveling. Most people wanted to board the plane, recline their seats, and take a nap.

The flight attendant began the safety briefing and as usual, virtually no one paid attention. She proceeded through the demonstration, and eventually we left the ground for what we hoped would be a boring, uneventful flight.

After the plane reached a comfortable cruising altitude, the attendant resumed her duties of reminding passengers of additional safety precautions by saying, "Ladies and gentlemen, welcome again to USAirways flight number 1262, *hopefully* nonstop service to Charlotte, North Carolina!" She immediately had our attention. She continued, "We are currently cruising at an altitude of 33,000 feet. I remind you that this has been designated a nonsmoking flight. The restrooms have been equipped with smoke detectors for your safety. Anyone caught smoking in the aircraft lavatory or tampering with a smoke detector will be issued a federal fine...and *asked to step outside!*"

For the remainder of that flight, like E.F. Hutton, whenever she spoke, we listened and we listened good. Why? Because for a brief moment in time she chose to incorporate some humor into the workplace. She chose to do things differently, and that evening when we arrived into Charlotte, everyone leaving the plane had a smile on his or her face. One person made the difference in the lives of everyone on that aircraft.

Sometimes we get caught in the frame of mind that I'm just one person and I can't make a difference. But if everyone would consciously make the effort to put a smile on his or her face and once per day make another laugh, we could all reduce stress.

President Clinton and his wife Hillary were on vacation in Little Rock, Arkansas, when the President realized that they were low on gas and pulled into a local service station. Mr. Clinton drove into the full-service island where the service attendant was one of his wife's ex-boyfriends. Mr. Clinton began to laugh. He turned to his wife and said, "Hillary, if you had married him, you would be the wife of a gas station attendant!" Mrs. Clinton quickly turned to her husband and said, "No, Bill, if I had married him, he would be the President of the United States!"

Everybody, no matter how young or old, goes through tremendous changes in their lives on a daily basis.

One of the greatest things that ever happened in my life is the fact that I found someone willing to marry me. My wife, Rozanne, is 5' 9" tall and I am only 5' 7". This difference in height has made me the butt of numerous jokes from family and friends, but I always tell her, "Honey, it is better to have loved a short man than to never have loved a-tall."

Rozanne did an outstanding job planning our wedding, and everything was perfect. She picked out the dresses and tuxedos, decided on flowers and boutonnieres, chose the decorations for the reception, and hired a band. She was highly organized and the day went off with only one "hitch" (that was to me).

One evening, prior to the wedding, Rozanne and I, along with her parents, were discussing when photos were to be taken. We were planning a traditional wedding where the day of the ceremony the bride and groom were not supposed to see one another until she came walking down the aisle to pomp and circumstance. We discussed having all photos taken after the ceremony, however she was concerned that following the wedding the women's makeup would be messy because of the ceremonial crying and blubbering that most women do at weddings. Of course, we couldn't take pictures together before the wedding because that would break tradition, so Rozanne decided to have her photos taken separately with the bridesmaids, groomsmen, and parents before the ceremony. Next she would return to a room in the back of the church, and I would come out and go through the same procedure.

The conversation became a heated debate as each one of us expressed our own ideas of how things should be done. In no little frustration, I finally asked, "What's all this about women crying? This is supposed to be a happy occasion. When am I supposed to cry?" Without one moment's hesitation Rozanne said, "For the rest of your life." Immediately, we all broke into laughter! The stressful situation had been defused, and very quickly the plans for taking pictures fell into place.

WHO PACKS THE PARACHUTE?

Again, humor made the difference!

Try a bit of the unexpected in the workplace. I'm not suggesting that we create a circus environment but one that is a pleasure to be a part of. One Saturday morning my mother, the mother of seven children, was preparing breakfast in the kitchen. My father walked into the room and noticed that her hair was frazzled and she was wearing that old flannel nightgown that is passed from generation to generation. He smiled, laughed, and said, "Good morning mother of seven!" She replied, "Good morning, father of three!" Laughter filled the house. My father didn't get mad--although he was speechless for a period of time. Our home was always filled with laughter and good times. Yes, we had tough times, but my parents chose to concentrate on the treasures of life. We laughed, not at one another, but at the humor that surrounds us each and every day and tried to find humor in what could be trying situations.

Show me a house filled with laughter and I'll show you a home filled with love.

I'm not trying to make anyone mad, upset, or frustrated by these stories, but to make us laugh and think about life itself. Occasionally, I meet people who are so pessimistic and have such "thin skin" that they are constantly waiting for me to say something that makes them angry. We all know people like this--they can be so bitter about life that they make everyone miserable.

I met a teacher who never attended high school football games. When I inquired as to why, he said, "I know that every time they get into a huddle, they're talking about me!" Even in the bitterness of others, in many instances, there is humor for the rest of us.

We are surrounded by humor each and every day. On May 17, 1992, I was driving to a presentation and listening to a talk radio station. The program to which I was listening was interrupted for an announcement. The DJ broke in to inform the listening audience of the death of a very beloved entertainer. In a deep, depressed, and sorrow-filled voice he said, "Ladies and gentlemen, it saddens me to share with you the following report. One of America's premier entertainers has passed away. This gentleman brought beautiful music to the entire world and maintained his longtime popularity with a musical style of "champagne music" that seemed to satisfy a widespread interest in nostalgia. He earned his first accordion by hiring himself out as a farm laborer and formed his own dance band at the age of 17.

"Millions of people have grown up listening to his records and watching his television show, which aired from 1955 through 1982. This man made the "bubble machine" famous. Yes, ladies and gentlemen, Lawrence Welk passed away today, he was 89 *degrees* (pause). Years old! Years old! He was 89 years old! #*%*! I'm sorry, he was 89 years old." With that he signed off and the radio went silent.

I could imagine that numerous people like myself, heard this eulogy and laughed as they drove. Not only did Lawrence Welk bring joy to hearts when he was living but in a strange sort of way humor in his passing. (Isn't it interesting that some of our most embarrassing moments become some of our fondest memories?) My hope is that when I pass, somebody gets a laugh out of it, (besides my wife as she cashes the life insurance check) or a memory brings a smile to someone's face.

When Rozanne and I were single, we did things with single people. After we got married we started doing things with married couples, and now that we have children, we seem to have drifted to doing things with couples with children. It is kind of a natural transition that we all go through.

One of my "hobbies" is observing people, and I have noticed that some of my married friends' wives have begun to get a little bit "healthier." I posed the question to my wife one day, "Rozanne, why is it that single women are thinner than married women?" She said, "It's simple. Single women come home, see what's in the refrigerator and go to bed. Married women come home, see what's in bed, and go to the refrigerator!" Needless to say, I don't ask too many questions around the house anymore!

For our first wedding anniversary I decided I wanted to do something different. Having addressed hundreds of groups and discussed the importance of trying things that are new, of being open to positive change, I decided to practice what I preach. A gift for my new bride had to be something original. Flowers were too common, jewelry would be expected, and I didn't want to take her to some fancy restaurant like...the Waffle House. For weeks I pondered over what to get my darling wife. Finally, one evening while watching a movie on television, it hit me.

We were watching a movie starring Patrick Swazye and Keanu Reeves called *Point Break*. During this movie they go sky diving. My wife said, "You know, I've always wanted to go sky diving." I said, "You want to jump out of a perfectly good airplane?" She replied, "It's always been a dream of mine."

Rozanne is a very adventuresome individual. She has been whitewater rafting and parasailing, traveled to the bottom of the Grand Canyon, and snorkeled in the Bahamas. Therefore, I decided I'd surprise her. We live in Charlotte, North Carolina, and the following Monday morning I phoned a company in Chester, South Carolina, called Skydive Carolina. I made an appointment to go sky diving the Saturday morning following our first anniversary. I told my wife nothing about it (it was to be totally unexpected). I informed her that we were going to a local park for a picnic with friends. On Saturday morning the alarm clock went off, I got dressed, and hurried downstairs to wait for Rozanne. Eventually, she came downstairs, looking quite lovely in a sundress.

Now, the thought of my new bride, free-falling from an airplane with her sundress billowed around her head, didn't seem appropriate. I convinced her to change and we left for the "park." We traveled down Interstate 77 to Chester, South Carolina and turned off the "hard road" onto an unpaved, unmowed "pig-trail." There at the end was the airport. My wife saw the Skydive Carolina sign and was enthusiastic about the activities yet to come.

The airport consists of a doublewide mobile home and a grass strip. The mobile home is the airtraffic control tower, training facility, snack bar, and tanning salon. When we registered inside, the receptionist informed us that our training would begin as soon as the pilot finished mowing the runway. I began to wonder if I would live to see our second anniversary.

Eventually, our instructor Steve Vaughn came in and introduced himself. We were then escorted, along with numerous other "first-timers," to a back room for instruction. We were informed of what was expected from each of us and what we were to expect from the instructors, discussed the safety aspects of skydiving, viewed several videos that discussed the intricate details of skydiving, were introduced to the equipment, given a description of what to expect, and asked if we had any questions.

My question, of course, was, "Who packs the parachute?" His reply, "You do!"

Now, never having packed a parachute in my life, I realized that the instructor knew the secret to my success, so therefore I followed every direction exactly as it was given.

Eventually, we, along with other first-timers and professionals, boarded our aircraft--a 1942 Beechcraft. I wasn't even born until 1962, so you can imagine my concern. The plane leapt down that grassy runway and took off. We climbed to our maximum cruising altitude of 10,500 feet. The professionals exited the plane and created fancy formations by grabbing ankles and elbows. Now it was time for the first-timers to jump! I have never been so embarrassed in my life. To see a grown man, standing at the door of that aircraft, whimpering, crying, whining, and acting like such a weenie! They finally got ME quiet, however, and we exited the plane. There I was, free-falling from 10,500 feet at approximately 120 miles per hour and, thanks to my mother, the only thing I could think was "In case I have an accident, I hope I have on clean underwear!" Eventually I pulled the ripcord and the parachute opened perfectly.

I began to wonder, how many people follow the same ruts and routines day in and day out. How many of us fail to create our future and merely stand by and watch things happen. I'm not saying that we must all go bungy-cord jumping or, heaven forbid, jump out of a perfectly good airplane. What I am saying is that we are responsible for our futures. We are responsible for ourselves and where we will end up in life. This means that we must open our minds to the tremendous opportunities that surround us each and every day of our lives because the decisions we make today will directly impact our lives tomorrow.

Our minds are like parachutes...they only work when they're open. Let's expand our horizons, demand the best out of life, and celebrate the many blessings we have been so graciously given. *You and I are responsible for packing our own parachutes and those of our children and associates for their free-fall into life.* Let's do a better than terrific job!

I wish you all the best,
Patrick

P.S.   Rozanne thoroughly enjoyed the experience of skydiving and looks forward to her next opportunity to free-fall.

MORE
ABOUT
PATRICK

PATRICK T. GRADY

Thousands of individuals throughout North America have been inspired and motivated by Patrick's fast-paced and lighthearted messages. Through the use of humor he is able to capture the audience's attention and "hold them in the palm of his hand." Patrick's spirited and enthusiastic delivery, message, humor, substance and personal insights are excellent and make a lasting impression upon those attending his presentations. He has the unique ability to motivate, inspire and communicate to his audiences the qualities needed to keep both their professional and personal lives growing in a positive direction. If you are looking for a speaker for your next conference or meeting, Patrick is "*just* what the doctor ordered!"

Patrick's personalized presentations address topics such as:

♦ Putting humor back into the workplace
♦ Positive mental attitude
♦ Being open to positive change
♦ Creating a new enthusiasm for your work
♦ Providing superior customer service
♦ Handling rejection
♦ Building client relationships
♦ Creative leadership
♦ Preparing for and creating futures
♦ Building team spirit
♦ Overcoming adversity
♦ Motivation
♦ Reducing stress
♦ Goal setting
♦ The dangers of drugs, alcohol and tobacco

For further information on booking Patrick for your next conference or meeting, contact:

"TNT" Enterprises, Inc.
(800) 862-1660

To receive additional copies of

WHO PACKS THE PARACHUTE

**Video, cassette tapes, or
compact discs, contact:**

"TNT" **ENTERPRISES, INC.**

AT

(800) 862-1660

**QUANTITY DISCOUNTS
ARE AVAILABLE.**

NOTES

NOTES

NOTES

NOTES

NOTES

NOTES